AT THE TABLE OF ISRAEL

SANDY LESBERG

At The Table Of
ISRAEL

A Unique Collection of Three Hundred
Traditional and Modern Israeli Recipes

The Bobbs-Merrill Company : Peebles Press
INDIANAPOLIS : NEW YORK

At The Table Of Israel by Sandy Lesberg
ISBN 0-672 51766-3
Library of Congress Catalogue Card Number 72-89704

Decorations by
AUDREY ORRIDGE

Printed and bound in Great Britain

This book is for Golda Meir,
with respect

INTRODUCTION

In the beginning. . . .

The beginning was 1948. Before the existence of modern Israel Jews exulted in survival by the grace of all the other peoples of the world. 1948 began a new way of life for the oldest civilized people on earth. When the history of Judaism is recounted many centuries from now, the year 1948 will be noted as the time when the Jews decided that even though their history might have been in the hands of others, their destiny was strictly a matter of their own doing. When the existence of the new State of Israel was declared to the world, it was much more than a political pronouncement. Inherent in the words of national independence was the unspoken commitment of the founding citizens to banish forever from the hearts of Jews everywhere the one over-riding deleterious psychological characteristic that found them huddled under the same shadow no matter where they lived—the shadow of fear.

No more would any Jew have to fear the displeasure of his neighbor —no more the fear of being derided as a second class citizen, deported as an undesirable element, deprived of worldly goods and station and moral stature by the whim and rule of an unconscienced majority in search of a scapegoat. No more would any Jew have to fear for his life or the lives of his family as a result of a political or religious movement in search of new conquests under the devil's banner.

The history of the world will record 1948 as the time when all Jews came home—some physically, most spiritually. Some in the time of battle, most in the comfort of joining an established process. Remember, the Israeli law of return states that any Jew in the world can become a citizen of Israel.

Religiously they decided that a truly holy man did his own just bidding under the umbrella blessing of a wise supportive God. Politically they realized that they must declare the country free and independent, establish as viable a defense perimeter as was possible, and prepare for a war of birth or death. Realistically, they understood that they must make their own way against the diplomatic and military might of their immediate neighbors who were actively hostile and determined to pursue a policy of annihilation, and against the more distant observer countries who were less hostile than they were displeased at the audacity of the Jews in presuming to become the masters of their own fate after five thousand years of being the creatures of these same great observer powers.

Above all, there was no self-delusion. The world's sympathy is extended to a Jew in trouble. Tears are shed and hands outstretched in direct proportion to his plight. But when he stands erect and declares his active participation in the grand human design based on God's mandate for all people, he is vilified for his impunity and his friends in adversity unify to become his enemies in life. So above all, the founding fathers of Israel enunciated the startling maxim that is destined to remove from Jews everywhere the extraordinary anti-life psychological burden that before 1948 seemed to be their heritage.

Simply stated, the people of Israel don't care if they are liked or not, don't care if they are accepted or not, praised condemned applauded vilified—it matters not a whit so long as the sanctity of their national identity as the State of Israel is maintained. This is true of all Jews. Everywhere. The State of Israel is the living salvation of every Jew who has ever faced a hostile act impelled by the fact of his being Jewish. It is true for the most influential in the most affluent enlightened society and it is true for a Russian Jew despairing of his religious and political freedom. It is true for the oppressed and for the liberated. This is the meaning of 1948.

Why, then, a cookbook? The strength of Israel is her people and I was determined to know them and to share with them their unique celebration of life. I am convinced that the culture of any land is most readily grasped by the table they prepare, and in Israel, as in Jewish homes everywhere, the tradition of celebration leads to the table. For me the great fascination was in the diversity of foods that I found. Jews from Algeria prepare their goulash with couscous, Moroccan Jews stuff their chicken with pomegranates, avocados are stuffed, shredded, baked, broiled, etc. Wherever the people of Israel began their journey, they carried their national dishes with them and now they are all a part of the table of Israel.

Here, then, are three hundred recipes that illuminate the culture of this young nation. There is purity in their varied backgrounds and there is strength in the sameness of their purpose. And as this is no ordinary cookbook, even though the recipes are fascinating in themselves, I have chosen to illustrate them with pictures of the people rather than with pictures of the food. For this book is, above all, a celebration of the people.

Sandy Lesberg

CONTENTS

SALADS
and
APPETIZERS

Herring Marinated in Cognac

2 plump herring
3 medium onions
⅓ cup cognac
Juice of 1 lemon
½ teaspoon sugar

2 tablespoons oil
Pinch of black pepper
Pinch of dry mustard
¼ teaspoon paprika
1 bay leaf

Peel and bone the fish. Divide into pieces. Slice the onion into thin rings and place in a container with the fish sections. Combine the remaining ingredients and pour over the fish mixture. Allow to marinate at least 2 hours before serving.

Serves: 4

Herring with Apples

6 salt herring
1 cup apples, cubed
1 cup onions, chopped
½ cup cucumber pickles, cubed
1 cup sugar
3 tablespoons oil

1 cup vinegar
1 teaspoon mustard
1 cup tomato purée
1 bay leaf
½ teaspoon celery salt

Soak fish in water overnight. Remove skin and bones. Cut into chunks. Add the remaining ingredients, mixing thoroughly. Place in a closed container and refrigerate.

Serves: 6

Salt Herring in Cream

3 large salt herring   ¼ teaspoon black pepper
3 slices white bread, soaked in   ¼ teaspoon paprika
water and squeezed dry   Pinch of cinnamon
3 eggs, beaten   1 tablespoon butter, softened
½ teaspoon onion salt   ¾ cup cream

Soak fish in water overnight. Remove the skin and bones and grind the fish and bread together. Add the eggs, onion salt, pepper, paprika and cinnamon, blending thoroughly. Beat in the butter and cream. Pour the prepared mixture into a greased baking tin. Bake in a medium oven (350°) for 1 hour. Accompany with boiled potatoes.

Serves: 6

Salt Herring and Olive Spread

2 salt herring   ½ cup oil
3 ounces (90 grams) large   2 teaspoons wine vinegar
black olives   ½ teaspoon mustard
1 stick (125 grams) butter   1 bay leaf

Soak the herring in water overnight. Clean, skin and bone the fish. Remove the pits from the olives and grind the fish and olives together 3 times. Add the butter and grind again. Incorporate the remaining ingredients and mix well. Refrigerate for 24 hours.

Serves: 4

Spicy Salad (Orange and Olive)

2 oranges
½ cup black olives, sliced
½ cup green olives, sliced
¼ teaspoon salt

Pinch of cayenne pepper
1 tablespoon oil
2 tablespoons kirsch

Peel the oranges and cut into small sections. Combine with the olives. Add the salt, pepper and oil. Sprinkle with kirsch. Chill.

Serves: 4

Olive and Pimiento Spread

½ cup boiling water
¼ cup soybean flour
1 teaspoon soy sauce
1 tablespoon green olives, chopped
1 tablespoon black olives, chopped
1 pimiento, finely chopped

2 tablespoons mayonnaise
1 tablespoon soybean oil
½ teaspoon mustard
1 tablespoon parsley, finely chopped
1 clove garlic, crushed
Salt and pepper to taste

Add boiling water to flour in the top of a double boiler and blend well. Cook for 10 minutes, stirring occasionally. Let cool. Add the remaining ingredients and blend until smooth.

Serves: 2

Spicy Tomatoes

6 tomatoes
¾ cup parsley, finely chopped
2 cloves garlic, finely chopped
1 teaspoon onion, finely chopped

¼ teaspoon salt
¼ teaspoon black pepper
1 teaspoon lemon juice
¼ teaspoon spicy mustard
3 tablespoons oil

Cut the tomatoes in half and scoop out the seeds. Combine the parsley, garlic, onion, salt, pepper, lemon juice and mustard and spread the resulting mixture over the tomato halves. Sauté in 3 tablespoons oil, filled side up. Arrange tomatoes in a shallow baking dish and bake 15 minutes in a hot oven (400°). Serve hot or cold.

Serves: 6

Melon Cups

3 cantaloupes
¾ cup rice, boiled
¾ cup dates, pitted and chopped
The flesh of 2 avocados, thinly sliced
1 cup walnuts, shelled
¼ cup green olives, diced

¼ cup black olives, diced
¼ teaspoon salt
1 tablespoon oil
1 tablespoon lemon juice
12 leaves Boston (Great Lake) lettuce
6 sprigs mint

Cut the cantaloupes in half and remove the seeds. Scoop out the flesh with a spoon, leaving the shells intact. Cube the flesh and combine it with the rice, dates and avocado slices. Gently incorporate the nuts and diced olives. Season with salt, oil and lemon juice. Line each melon shell with 2 lettuce leaves and fill with the prepared mixture. Garnish with mint sprigs.

Serves: 6

Vegetable Salad with *Burghul*

1 cup finely milled *burghul* (buckwheat groats)	½ teaspoon salt
1 cucumber, sliced	¼ teaspoon black pepper
2 radishes, sliced	½ teaspoon cinnamon
1 scallion (shallot), sliced	3 tablespoons olive oil
1 small green pepper, cut into strips	1 tablespoon lemon juice
	8 lettuce leaves
	2 tomatoes, sliced

1½ hours before preparing the salad, rinse *burghul* well. Let stand. Combine the prepared vegetables. Season with salt, pepper and cinnamon. Dress with oil and lemon juice. Incorporate the *burghul* and mound on lettuce leaves. Garnish with tomato slices.

Serves: 2

Pickled Eggplant

3 eggplants	½ teaspoon ground cloves
Oil for frying	2 teaspoons celery seed
1 hot green pepper, cut into strips	Vinegar
4 cloves garlic, chopped	Water

Rinse the eggplants well and cut into strips ½-inch thick. Sauté in oil until soft but not limp. Set aside to cool.

Transfer the strips to a flat glass dish or container. Stir in the green pepper, garlic, cloves and celery seed. Cover with a mixture of vinegar and water (¾ cup water per cup of vinegar). Refrigerate for 2 days before serving.

Serves: 4-6

Avocado Salad in *Tehina**

1 ripe avocado
2 tablespoons lemon juice
½ teaspoon salt
¼ teaspoon paprika
1 tablespoon green olives,
chopped

1 tablespoon parsley, chopped
1 onion, minced
Tehina (see below)
Black olives

Press the avocado flesh through a fine strainer. Add the lemon juice, salt, paprika, olives, parsley and onion. Blend well. Complete preparation of the semi-prepared *tehina* (see below) and add to the avocado mixture. Garnish with black olives.

To prepare *Tehina*:

4 tablespoons semi-prepared
tehina
Juice of 1 lemon

½ cup water
½ teaspoon salt
5 garlic cloves, crushed

Blend together the semi-prepared *tehina* and the lemon juice. Add water, bit by bit, until the resulting mixture has the consistency of sour cream. Use more water if necessary. Add salt and garlic.

Serves: 2

*A paste made of crushed sesame seeds, available at specialty shops in jars and cans in *semi-prepared* form.

Mixed Cabbage Salad

3 cups red cabbage, shredded
3 cups green cabbage, shredded
1 onion, sliced in rings
1 cup mayonnaise
1 teaspoon celery seed
¼ teaspoon sugar

1 teaspoon lemon juice
½ teaspoon salt
¼ teaspoon black pepper
1 cup black olives
3 cooked beets, sliced
2 tablespoons blanched almonds, slivered

Combine the cabbage and onion. Incorporate the mayonnaise, celery seed, sugar, lemon juice, salt and pepper, mixing well. Add the olives, beets and almonds. Toss gently.

Serves: 4-6

Rice and Peanuts in Soy Sauce

3 cups rice
6 cups salted water
4 scallions (shallots)
¼ cup margarine

½ cup salted peanuts, chopped
¼ cup parsley, chopped
1 tablespoon soy sauce

Cook the rice in salted water. Remove from heat before it softens completely (about 20 minutes). Drain. Let stand until the rice dries.

Chop the scallions and sauté in margarine until well browned. Add the chopped peanuts and cooked rice. Mix well and stir in the parsley and soy sauce. Continue cooking until the rice is completely soft.

Serves: 12

Burghul Patties Stuffed with Meat

¼ cup currants
1 pound (500 grams) *burghul* (buckwheat groats)
2 cups water
7 ounces (210 grams) semolina
1½ teaspoons salt
3 scallions (shallots)
½ pound (250 grams) lean lamb

Oil for frying
1 tablespoon parsley, chopped
½ teaspoon black pepper
½ teaspoon cardamon
3 tablespoons tomato paste
Chicken stock
¼ teaspoon oregano

Soak the currants for 30 minutes in water to cover. Drain.

Soak the *burghul* in 2 cups water for 10 minutes. Add the semolina and ½ teaspoon salt and knead into a dough. Let stand for 15 minutes.

Chop the scallions and sprinkle with ½ teaspoon salt. Dice the meat. Squeeze the moisture out of the scallions. Heat the oil in a flameproof casserole and sauté the scallions. Add the parsley, currants, pepper and cardamon. Cook, stirring constantly, for 5 minutes. Add the meat and continue cooking and stirring until the meat is tender. Set aside to cool.

Divide the meat and *burghul* into an equal number of portions. Form the *burghul* into patties and fill with the meat mixture. Seal closed.

Heat the tomato paste thinned with chicken stock in a large saucepan. Add the remaining salt and the oregano. Bring to the boil. Arrange the patties in the casserole and cook for 10 minutes.

Remove the patties from the sauce, drain, sauté in oil and serve at once. Accompany with vegetable salad and pickles.

Serves: 4

Spicy Lamb and Nut Balls

1 pound (500 grams) finely milled *burghul* (buckwheat groats)	¼ teaspoon black pepper
2 cups flour	¾ cup oil
½ teaspoon salt	Water
	Oil for deep-frying

Soak the *burghul* in water to cover for several hours, changing the soaking liquid from time to time. Drain well. Add the flour, salt and pepper to the *burghul*. Work in the oil, moisten and knead into a dough.

Shape into balls. Press a hole into each with your finger and fill with the prepared filling. Seal the balls carefully. Deep-fry in hot oil.

Filling

1 medium onion, finely chopped	½ teaspoon cinnamon
2 scallions, finely chopped	¼ teaspoon cumin
3 tablespoons oil	2 tablespoons pine nuts
1 pound (500 grams) lean lamb, chopped	2 tablespoons walnuts, crushed
½ teaspoon salt	1 tablespoon raisins, finely chopped
¼ teaspoon black pepper	

Sauté the onion and scallions in oil until golden. Add the chopped meat, salt, pepper, cinnamon and cumin and brown well. Remove from flame. Mix in the pine nuts, walnuts and raisins.

Serves: 4

Beets in Sauce

4 medium beets	2 tablespoons tomato purée
3 eggs	1 teaspoon salt
2 tablespoons flour	1 teaspoon parsley, chopped
1 tablespoon bread crumbs	3 tablespoons oil

Grind the beets and combine with the eggs, flour, bread crumbs, tomato purée, salt and parsley. Shape the mixture into balls and sauté in oil. Simmer in the prepared sauce for ½ hour. Serve hot or cold.

Sauce

1 small onion, chopped	Juice of one lemon
1 tablespoon margarine	2½ cups water
1 cup tomato purée	½ teaspoon salt
2 tablespoons sugar	½ teaspoon black pepper
1 teaspoon prepared horse-radish	

Sauté the chopped onion in the margarine. Stir in the remaining ingredients and blend thoroughly.

Serves: 4

Falafel (Chick Pea Croquettes)

⅓ cup chick peas
¼ teaspoon baking soda
5 cloves garlic
1 teaspoon onion, minced
1 tablespoon parsley, chopped
¼ cup soybean flour
½ slice bread, soaked in water and squeezed dry

2 teaspoons baking powder
1 teaspoon lemon juice
1 teaspoon salt
1 teaspoon paprika
1 teaspoon cumin
Oil for deep-frying

Soak the chick peas and soda overnight in water to cover. Drain.

Put through the grinder with the garlic, onion and parsley. Add flour, bread, baking powder, lemon juice, salt, paprika and cumin. Combine well. Shape into balls and deep-fry in hot oil until golden.

Serves: 2

Spinach with Chick Peas

1 cup chick peas
¼ teaspoon baking soda
4 tablespoons oil
1 pound (500 grams) fresh spinach

½ teaspoon mustard
⅛ teaspoon nutmeg
½ teaspoon salt
1 teaspoon lemon juice

Soak the chick peas and soda overnight in water to cover. Rinse well, transfer to a saucepan and cover with fresh water. Add the oil and cook over a low flame until the chick peas are soft.

Rinse the spinach thoroughly, discard the stems and chop the leaves. Add to the chick peas and cook over a medium flame until the spinach is done, stirring occasionally. Add additional hot water if necessary.

Remove from heat, drain well and season with mustard, nutmeg, salt and lemon juice. Serve hot or cold.

Serves: 2

Asparagus Patties

2 pounds (1 kilogram) asparagus
½ cup cooked, cubed lamb
½ teaspoon rosemary
1 teaspoon salt
½ teaspoon black pepper
1 teaspoon onion, minced
2 eggs
¾ cup matzo meal
3 tablespoons oil

Trim, wash and dice the asparagus. Put the meat and the asparagus through a grinder. Combine the meat mixture, rosemary, salt, pepper, onion and eggs in a mixing bowl. Stir in the matzo meal. Shape into patties and fry in oil.

Serves: 6

Leek Patties

2 pounds (1 kilogram) leeks
1 onion
¾ cup water
2½ teaspoons salt
1 cup beef, ground
1 slice white bread, soaked in water and squeezed dry
2 eggs
¼ teaspoon black pepper
½ teaspoon rosemary
1 tablespoon parsley, chopped
1 egg, beaten
1 cup flour
3 tablespoons oil

Trim leeks, cut into large pieces and wash well. Cook in pressure cooker with onion, water and 2 teaspoons salt for 20 minutes. Drain well and put through a grinder with the meat and bread. Add the 2 eggs, the remaining salt, pepper, rosemary and parsley and combine thoroughly. Shape into patties, dip in beaten egg, then flour, and sauté on both sides in oil until golden.

Serve as a side dish.

Serves: 6

Vegetable Croquettes

1 pound (500 grams) carrots, grated
1 small onion, minced
1 scallion, minced
3 tablespoons oil
2 large potatoes, peeled and grated

2 tablespoons soybean flour
1 egg
½ teaspoon salt
½ teaspoon black pepper
½ teaspoon rosemary
1 tablespoon parsley, chopped

Place the carrots, onion and scallion in a saucepan with the unheated oil. Cook slowly until vegetables are soft. Remove to a mixing bowl. Stir in the remaining ingredients. Blend well. Form into medium-sized croquettes. Fry in hot oil.

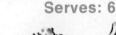

Serves: 6

Baked Corn Pudding

1 stick (125 grams) margarine
3 tablespoons flour
3 cups milk
¼ teaspoon paprika
2½ cups canned corn kernels, drained
2 egg yolks

1 pimiento, chopped
3 ounces (90 grams) cream cheese
¾ cup Gouda cheese, grated
1 teaspoon salt
2 egg whites, stiffly beaten

Melt half the margarine in a saucepan and quickly stir in the flour. Blend well. Add 1 cup milk, stirring constantly. When mixture is smooth, gradually incorporate the rest of the milk and the paprika, continuing to cook until thick. Remove from heat and cool.

Combine the corn with the egg yolks, pimiento, cream cheese, half the Gouda cheese and the salt. Stir into the milk mixture. Fold in the egg whites. Pour the pudding into a greased baking pan, sprinkle with the remaining Gouda cheese and margarine and bake in a medium oven (350°) for 1 hour.

Serves: 4-6

Sautéed Okra

2 cloves garlic, chopped
1 small onion, chopped
2 tablespoons oil
1 pound (500 grams) okra, sliced
1 small green pepper, seeded and diced

1 large tomato, chopped
¼ teaspoon black pepper
1 cup chicken stock
½ teaspoon salt
2 tablespoons lemon juice

Sauté the garlic and onion in oil until browned. Stir in the okra and green pepper. Add the tomato and black pepper. Moisten with boiling chicken stock. Cover and cook at low heat until okra is soft. Remove from flame and season with salt and lemon juice.

Serves: 4

Roast Vegetables

1 large onion
2 scallions (shallots)
6 carrots
1 head cauliflower
¼ head cabbage
3 large tomatoes
1 potato
1 green pepper
½ cup kidney beans

2 small squash
1 eggplant
4 tablespoons oil or margarine
1 teaspoon salt
½ teaspoon black pepper
2 teaspoons paprika
¼ cup parsley, chopped
¼ cup chives, chopped

Prepare and dice all the vegetables. Put the oil or margarine into a baking pan. Add the vegetables, salt, pepper and paprika, sprinkle with parsley and chives and roast in a low oven (275°) until the vegetables are soft (about 40 minutes).

Serves: 4

Cucumber Salad

6 cucumbers
2 tablespoons lemon juice
1 teaspoon oil
½ teaspoon salt

1 tablespoon dry mint leaves,
crushed
Black olives

Peel the cucumbers. Cut into thin slices. Dress with lemon juice, oil and salt. Sprinkle with mint leaves. Garnish with olives.

Serves: 8

Beet Salad

8 beets
¼ teaspoon black pepper
¼ teaspoon cumin
2 tablespoons vinegar
2 tablespoons oil

½ teaspoon salt
½ teaspoon mustard
2 cloves garlic, chopped
¼ cup parsley, chopped

Cook the unpeeled beets in boiling water until soft (about 1 hour). Peel and cut into strips. Season with pepper, cumin, vinegar, oil, salt and mustard. Sprinkle with chopped garlic and parsley. Refrigerate.

Serves: 6

Green Pepper and Cognac Salad

6 large green peppers	½ cup cognac
6 scallions (shallots)	3 tablespoons sweetened lemon juice
5 tablespoons oil	
1 teaspoon salt	2 tablespoons natural lemon juice
1 small hot pepper, thinly sliced	

Cut the peppers and scallions into thin rings. Sauté the scallions in hot oil until the layers separate. Cover and cook for a few minutes longer over a low heat. Add the green peppers and a pinch of salt.

Stir lightly. Continue cooking for 5 minutes, stirring from time to time. Add the hot pepper, cognac, lemon juice and remaining salt. Mix well and cook for an additional 5 minutes. Cover the pan and remove from heat. Allow to cool. Transfer to a glass jar. Refrigerate.

Serves: 6

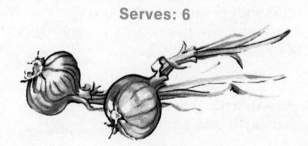

Avocado and Fruit Salad with Curry Dressing

1 grapefruit	¼ pound (125 grams) white grapes
2 tangerines	
3 pineapple rings, canned	Vinaigrette dressing
A ½-pound (250 gram) avocado	Curry powder to taste
	Sugar to taste

Peel the grapefruit and tangerines and divide into sections. Separate the pineapple rings into small pieces. Pare the avocado and cut it into strips the size of the fruit sections.

Combine the grapefruit, tangerines, pineapple and avocado. Stir in the grapes. Dress with vinaigrette, seasoned to taste with curry and sugar. Chill and serve.

Serves: 6

Vegetable and Fruit Table

This attractive addition to a buffet table can be presented on a single, large tray garnished with black olives, or as a series of separate salads. Amounts of ingredients required will depend on the number of guests to be served.

Fennel	Tomatoes
Raisins	Capers
Celery seed	Curry powder
Lemon juice	Onion
Olive oil	Chopped pimientos
Sugar	Salt
Tangerine	Tangerine juice
Mayonnaise	Cucumbers
Red wine	Cream
Cinnamon	Celery root
Chopped almonds or walnuts	Apple
Leeks	Anis seeds
Sliced black olives	Vermouth
Lime juice	Whole black olives
Chopped chives	

Grate the fennel, add raisins and season with celery seed, lemon juice, olive oil and a pinch of sugar.

Divide the tangerine into sections and dress with a mixture of mayonnaise, red wine and cinnamon. Sprinkle with chopped nuts.

Slice the leeks. Add sliced black olives. Season with lime juice, olive oil and chopped chives.

Slice the tomatoes and sprinkle with capers. Season with oil and curry.

Slice the onion in rings. Sprinkle with chopped pimientos. Dress with olive oil, salt, and tangerine juice.

Slice the cucumbers and combine with cream, a pinch of sugar and lime juice. Sprinkle with chopped chives.

Grate the celery root and apple. Add chopped nuts and anis seeds. Season with vermouth and mayonnaise.

Avocados in Wine

3 avocados
½ cup dry red wine
½ cup sugar
½ teaspoon lemon juice
Mint leaves

Cut the avocados in half and remove their pits.

Combine the wine, sugar and lemon juice. Blend thoroughly. Pour into the prepared avocado halves.

Garnish with mint leaves and serve over crushed ice.

Serves: 6

Tomatoes Stuffed with Curried Beef Salad

8 tomatoes
1½ cups lean beef, cooked and diced
¼ cup fennel, diced
2 tablespoons sweet red pepper, diced
1 cucumber pickle, diced
1 hard-cooked egg, chopped
½ teaspoon salt
¼ teaspoon black pepper
Mayonnaise
Curry powder
Chopped parsley

Carefully scoop out the tomatoes, leaving the cases intact. Reserve.

Combine the beef, fennel, red pepper, pickle and hard-cooked egg in a mixing bowl. Season with salt and pepper. Moisten with mayonnaise, flavored with curry powder to taste.

Fill the reserved tomato cases with the prepared beef salad. Chill. Sprinkle with chopped parsley and serve at once.

Serves: 8

Eggplant Salad with Cheese

½ pound (250 grams) small eggplants
½ pound (250 grams) Feta cheese
1 scallion, minced
4 cloves garlic, minced
3 pimientos, chopped
2 tablespoons green olives, chopped

1 tablespoon lemon juice
3 tablespoons oil
½ teaspoon salt
⅛ teaspoon black pepper
Lettuce leaves
Chopped parsley

Place the eggplants in a large frying pan and heat, turning them from side to side, until they are tender. Peel and mash in a large mixing bowl. Add the cheese, scallion, garlic, pimientos and olives. Dress with lemon juice, oil, salt and black pepper. Chill.

Garnish individual bowls with lettuce leaves. Fill with the eggplant mixture. Sprinkle with chopped parsley. Serve at once.

Serves: 4

B

Persimmons Stuffed with Cheese

3 persimmons
1 cup cottage cheese
2 tablespoons pine nuts, toasted

2 tablespoons figs, chopped
¼ cup sugar
1 teaspoon cinnamon

Cut the persimmons in half. Remove the seeds and rinse thoroughly. Combine the remaining ingredients, mixing well. Fill the persimmon halves with the prepared mixture and chill.

Serves: 6

Sweetbread Salad

¾ cup sweetbreads, boiled, cooked and diced
1 cup chicken, cooked and diced
½ cup fennel, diced

¼ cup sweet red pepper, diced
3 gherkins, sliced
1 teaspoon capers
Mayonnaise
Lettuce leaves

Combine the sweetbreads, chicken, fennel, red pepper, gherkins and capers in a large mixing bowl. Moisten with mayonnaise. Chill.

Serve in individual bowls garnished with lettuce leaves.

Serves: 4

Summer Squash Salad

2 pounds (1 kilogram) summer squash
2 tablespoons sweet red pepper, chopped
1 teaspoon onion, minced
2 stalks fennel, chopped

¼ cup small mushrooms, washed and trimmed
Mayonnaise
Prepared horseradish
Lettuce leaves
Chopped chives

Peel and dice the squash. Place in a metal colander, set over a pan of boiling water. Steam the squash until tender. Set aside to cool.

Add the red pepper, onion, fennel and mushrooms to the steamed squash. Dress with mayonnaise, seasoned with horseradish to taste. Chill.

To serve, mound on a bed of lettuce leaves and sprinkle with chopped chives.

Serves: 6

Curried Avocado and Eggplant Spread

3 eggplants, peeled
2 avocados, peeled and scooped
6 hard-cooked egg yolks (3 hard-cooked eggs may be substituted)
2 teaspoons oil

1 teaspoon lemon juice
1 teaspoon onion, minced
½ teaspoon salt
Curry powder
Paprika
Raisins

Mash the eggplants, avocados and eggs. Add the oil, lemon juice and onion. Blend thoroughly. Season with salt and curry powder to taste.

Place the spread in a glass serving dish, sprinkle with paprika and stud with raisins. Accompany with freshly-baked bread or crisp crackers.

Serves: 6

Tangy Avocado Purée

2 avocados	3 cloves garlic, minced
5 ounces (150 grams) Mozzarella cheese	1 teaspoon salt
	½ teaspoon black pepper
3 tablespoons prepared *tehina* (for preparation see page 20)	Juice of 1 lime

Mix the avocado and cheese in a blender. Add the remaining ingredients and mix thoroughly. Serve in individual dishes.

A tasty variation of this recipe can be prepared as follows:

2 avocados	Dash of Worcestershire sauce
1 small can green peas, drained	1 tablespoon pimiento, finely chopped
3 tablespoons prepared *tehina* (for preparation see page 20)	

Blend the avocado and peas in a blender or an electric mixer. Incorporate the *tehina,* combining thoroughly, then mix in the remaining ingredients.

Serves: 4

Carrot Relish

1 pound (500 grams) carrots	½ teaspoon cinnamon
Chicken stock	½ teaspoon cumin
½ cup vinegar	⅛ teaspoon cayenne pepper
¼ cup oil	¼ teaspoon salt
6 cloves garlic, chopped	1 teaspoon lemon rind, grated

Peel the carrots, place in a saucepan and cook in boiling chicken stock until tender. Drain.

Cut the carrots into thin slices. Return to the saucepan and add the remaining ingredients. Bring to the boil. Cook for 10 minutes. Set aside to cool. Store in a sealed jar.

Serves: 6

Pickled Avocado

6 cups water	2 pounds (1 kilogram) small,
3 tablespoons coarse (kosher)	unpeeled avocados, cut into
salt	chunks
1 teaspoon vinegar	½ teaspoon celery seed
2 tablespoons sweet red pepper,	¼ teaspoon ginger
chopped	2 tablespoons horseradish root,
8 cloves garlic	grated

Bring the water to the boil. Add the salt and boil for 5 minutes. Stir in the vinegar, red pepper and garlic. Remove from the flame.

Place the avocado chunks in a jar. Cover with the vinegar water. Add the celery seed, ginger and horseradish root.

Seal the jar with paraffin. Store for 7 days before serving.

Serves: 8

Eggplant and Pickle Rolls

1 large eggplant	1 teaspoon prepared horseradish
Salt	A few drops lemon juice
6 tablespoons flour	4 tablespoons mayonnaise
½ cup water	6 sour pickles
1 egg	Lettuce leaves
½ teaspoon salt	Tomato slices
¼ teaspoon black pepper	Stuffed green olives
Oil for deep-frying	

Peel the eggplant and slice into large rounds. Salt and let stand after drying thoroughly.

Dilute the flour in ½ cup water. Add the egg, salt and pepper. Combine well. Coat the eggplant slices with this batter and deep-fry them in hot oil. Set aside to cool.

Incorporate the horseradish and lemon juice into the mayonnaise.

Dice the pickles. Spread the pickle bits over the eggplant slices. Roll each slice up and fasten it with a toothpick.

Place the eggplant rolls on a bed of lettuce leaves. Spoon the mayonnaise over them. Garnish the platter with tomato slices and stuffed green olives.

Serves: 4

Jellied Avocados

1 package gelatin, unflavored	1 green pepper, seeded and diced
⅓ cup boiling water	½ teaspoon scallion, minced
3 avocados	¼ teaspoon salt
1 tablespoon lemon juice	Worcestershire sauce
3 eggs, hard-cooked	Mayonnaise
1 pimiento, cut into thin strips	Capers

Dissolve the gelatin in boiling water. Set aside to cool.

Cut the avocados in half, lengthwise. Remove the stones and the flesh, leaving a ½-inch shell. Sprinkle the avocado cases with ½ the lemon juice.

Peel the eggs. Slice 1 of them to obtain 6 slices for garnishing. Reserve the egg slices and mash the remaining eggs with the avocado flesh. Add the pimiento, green pepper and scallion. Season with salt, Worcestershire sauce to taste and the remaining lemon juice.

Add ½ the prepared gelatin to the avocado mixture. Set the rest aside to chill.

Fill the avocado cases with the egg and avocado. Chill. When the reserved gelatin is firm, chop it and sprinkle over the avocado halves. Garnish each stuffed avocado with a reserved egg slice, topped by a dab of mayonnaise and crowned with a few capers.

Serves: 6

Avocado and Herring Salad

4 avocados
1 tablespoon lemon juice
½ pound (250 grams) matjes herring, cut into ½-inch-long pieces
1 cup celery, chopped
2 small onions, sliced

4 gherkins, sliced
2 tablespoons oil
1 tablespoon sweet red pepper, chopped
Watercress
Tomato wedges

Cut the avocados in half, lengthwise, remove the stones and carefully scoop out the meat. Reserve the cases.

Cut the avocado meat into ½-inch cubes. Sprinkle with lemon juice and combine with the herring, celery, onions and gherkins. Dress with oil and blend thoroughly.

Fill the reserved avocado cases with the above mixture. Sprinkle with chopped red pepper. Chill.

Serve the stuffed avocados on a bed of watercress. Garnish with tomato wedges.

Serves: 4

Avocado and Walnut Salad

1 large, ripe avocado	¼ teaspoon black pepper
Juice of 1 lime	1 tablespoon mayonnaise
1 small onion, chopped	1 tablespoon parsley, chopped
3 cucumber pickles, sliced	Pimiento strips
1 stalk celery, chopped	Green pepper strips
½ cup walnuts, shelled	Black olives
½ teaspoon salt	

Cube the avocado. Sprinkle with lime juice. Gently incorporate the onion, pickles, celery and walnuts. Season with salt and pepper. Mix in the mayonnaise, combining well. Chill.

Before serving, sprinkle with parsley. Garnish with pimiento and green pepper strips and whole black olives.

Serves: 2

Pineapple and Persimmon Cocktail

2 ripe pineapples, peeled and cubed	½ cup white grapes
	Salt
3 persimmons, peeled and cubed	Black pepper
3 avocados, peeled and cubed	Sugar
1 grapefruit, divided into sections	Lemon juice
	Lettuce leaves
2 tangerines, divided into sections	2 eggs, hard-cooked and sliced

Combine the fruit. Dress with salt, pepper, sugar and lemon juice to taste. Line a serving dish with lettuce leaves. Add the mixed fruit and garnish with egg slices.

Serves: 6

Tomatoes Stuffed with Avocado

8 tomatoes
3 avocados
1 teaspoon salt
½ teaspoon black pepper
1 teaspoon prepared
horseradish
1 tablespoon parsley, chopped
Mayonnaise

4 eggs, hard-cooked
1 pound (500 grams) Feta cheese
1 teaspoon onion, minced
8 black olives, pitted and chopped
Paprika
Watercress
Green olives

Hollow out the tomatoes, being careful to leave the cases intact. Reserve the pulp.

Peel the avocados and thoroughly blend the avocado flesh and tomato pulp together. Season with ½ the salt, ½ the pepper and the horseradish. Add the parsley and mix thoroughly. Moisten with mayonnaise. Stuff the tomato cases with the resulting mixture. Chill.

Slice the hard-cooked eggs in half, lengthwise. Remove and mash the yolks. Add the cheese, onion, remaining salt and pepper and the black olives. Blend thoroughly and return the egg yolk mixture to the whites. Sprinkle with paprika.

Line a serving platter with watercress. Place the remaining cheese mixture in a mound in center and surround with the stuffed eggs and tomatoes. Garnish with green olives.

Serves: 4

SOUPS

Acapulco Avocado Soup

7 cups chicken stock
3 avocados
Juice of ½ lime

Pinch of nutmeg
Salt and black pepper to taste

Heat the chicken stock. Cut the avocado meat into pieces and put it in a blender with the warm stock. Add the lime juice, nutmeg, salt and pepper to taste. Blend for 5 minutes. Refrigerate.

Serves: 8

Lemon-Flavored Chicken Soup

6 tablespoons rice
8 cups chicken stock
4 eggs
Juice of 2 lemons

½ teaspoon curry powder
1 tablespoon chervil, chopped
(optional)

Cook the rice in the stock until soft. Beat the eggs and add the lemon juice and curry. Blend well. Stir in a few tablespoons of stock and combine thoroughly. Add the egg mixture to the stock and stir for a few minutes over a low heat. Sprinkle with chervil. Serve at once.

Serves: 6

Green Soup

2 onions, chopped
1 stalk celery, finely diced
3 tablespoons oil
1 cup chicken stock
3 bunches parsley, washed and drained

1 pound (500 grams) fresh spinach, washed and drained
5 cups water
1 cup lemon juice
1 teaspoon salt
½ teaspoon black pepper

Sauté the onions and celery in a soup pot in 3 tablespoons oil. Add 1 cup chicken stock, the parsley and the spinach. Simmer gently for 5 minutes, or until the greens are cooked. Put the spinach mixture through a blender and return to the pot. Stir in 5 cups of water, the lemon juice, salt and pepper. Heat and serve at once.

Serves: 6

Fish and Wine Soup

4 slices dry toasted white bread
5 cloves garlic
2 ounces (60 grams) margarine
¼ cup parsley, finely chopped
2 tablespoons celery, finely chopped
1½ pounds (750 grams) haddock

2 cups dry white wine
2 cups water
½ teaspoon saffron
½ teaspoon salt
¼ teaspoon black pepper
1 bay leaf

Rub the pieces of toast with 1 clove garlic. Reserve. Chop the remaining garlic and sauté it in margarine in a deep frying pan with the chopped parsley and celery. Add the fish fillets and sauté lightly.

Remove the fish and reserve. Add wine and water to the pot and season with saffron, salt, pepper and bay leaf. Bring to the boil. Return the reserved fish to the pot and cook over a low flame for 5 minutes.

Cut the toast into pieces. Arrange the toast bits in the bottom of individual soup dishes and cover with the strained soup. Serve the pieces of fish separately.

Serves: 4

Minted Chicken Broth

2 carrots
5 stalks celery
1 bay leaf
1 teaspoon salt
½ teaspoon black pepper
2 tablespoons mint leaves, crushed

1 tablespoon parsley, crushed
1 tablespoon lemon juice
3 garlic cloves, crushed
2 pounds (1 kilogram) chicken backs, necks, wings and feet
2 quarts water

Place all the ingredients in a soup pot with 2 quarts water. Simmer for 2½ hours. Strain and serve.

Serves: 6

Corn Soup

1 can corn kernels
3 cups milk
½ teaspoon onion salt
¼ teaspoon black pepper
2 teaspoons sugar

2 tablespoons cornstarch
3 tablespoons water
1 tablespoon mayonnaise
2 tablespoons chives, chopped

Put the corn and ½ its can of water in the blender. Add 1 cup milk. Blend until thick.

Transfer the corn mixture to a saucepan. Add the remaining milk, the onion salt, pepper and sugar. Stir in the cornstarch, dissolved in 3 tablespoons water, and the margarine.

Warm over a low flame (do not boil), sprinkle with chives, and serve.

Serves: 3

Lentil Soup

1 tablespoon fresh coriander leaves	4 cups chicken stock
½ teaspoon salt	¼ teaspoon black pepper
1 tablespoon cumin	Pinch of cayenne pepper
6 cloves garlic	1 tablespoon flour, mixed with a little water
1 tablespoon oil	2 scallions (shallots)
2 cups lentils (soaked overnight in water)	1 tablespoon parsley, chopped

Mash the coriander, the salt, cumin and garlic together. Sauté in hot oil. Add the lentils and cover with boiling water. Cook until the water evaporates, then add more water. Add boiling water as needed, until the lentils soften.

Drain the lentils. Add the chicken stock. Season with the black and cayenne pepper and bring to the boil. Add the flour-water mixture. Stir until the soup thickens. Slice the scallions and add to the soup. Sprinkle with parsley. Serve.

Serves: 6

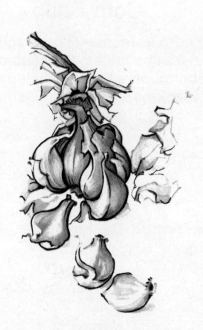

Spicy Orange and Lemon Soup

⅓ cup onion, finely chopped
2 tablespoons margarine
1 chicken bouillon cube
2 cups tomato juice

2 cups orange juice
1 cup lemon juice
1 lime, thinly sliced

Sauté the onion in margarine in a large saucepan until golden. Add the bouillon cube and tomato juice. Bring to the boil and cook, stirring constantly, until the bouillon cube dissolves. Add the orange and lemon juices and simmer over a low flame for 3 minutes. Garnish with lime slices. Serve at once.

Serves: 4

Squash Soup

1 pound (500 grams) squash, peeled and sliced
½ teaspoon salt
1 teaspoon sugar

4 cups chicken stock
1 egg, beaten
Juice of ½ lemon
Pinch of nutmeg

Place the squash in a saucepan. Season with salt and sugar and add chicken stock to cover. Reserve the rest of the stock. Cook over a medium flame until the squash is tender. Put through a food mill. Return to the saucepan, add the egg, mixed with lemon juice, and a pinch of nutmeg. Blend well. Stir in the remaining chicken stock. Serve hot or cold.

Serves: 6

Cucumber Soup

3 carrots, finely sliced
3 potatoes, peeled and sliced
¼ cup parsley, chopped
4 cups chicken stock

5 cucumbers, peeled and sliced
1 stalk fennel, diced
2 tablespoons margarine
½ pint sour cream

Cook the carrots, potatoes and parsley in chicken stock to cover until the vegetables are soft (about 20 minutes). Reserve the rest of the stock. Meanwhile sauté the cucumbers and fennel in the margarine. Place all the vegetables, the cooking liquid and the remaining chicken stock in the blender. Blend thoroughly. Transfer to a saucepan, heat over a medium flame, stir in the sour cream and serve at once.

Serves: 6

Onion Soup with Avocado

1 large onion, chopped
3 scallions (shallots), chopped
4 cloves garlic, chopped
Oil for frying
5 cups chicken stock
½ teaspoon salt

¼ teaspoon black pepper
⅛ teaspoon nutmeg
1 avocado, peeled and mashed
1 teaspoon lemon juice
A grating of lemon rind
1 egg yolk, beaten

Sauté the onion, scallions and garlic in oil until golden in a soup pot. Add the chicken stock and season with salt, pepper and nutmeg. Simmer for ½ hour.

Stir in the mashed avocado, lemon juice and lemon rind. Combine well. Add the egg yolk to the pot, blend it into the soup mixture, stirring constantly, and serve at once.

Serves: 6

Fish Soup Provençale

4 tomatoes, peeled	Celery leaves
6 cloves garlic	4 potatoes, diced
¾ cup oil	3 cups chicken stock
2 whites of leek, chopped	1½ teaspoons salt
2 scallions (shallots), chopped	½ teaspoon saffron
1 teaspoon orange rind, grated	3 pounds (1½ kilograms) 4 kinds
¼ cup parsley, chopped	fish (red snapper, halibut,
2 bay leaves	pompano, sea bass etc.)
1 tablespoon fennel, chopped	8 slices bread, toasted

Put the tomatoes, 4 cloves garlic, oil and leeks in the blender. Blend into a smooth paste.

Place the scallions, orange rind, parsley, bay leaves, fennel, celery leaves, potatoes and 3 cups chicken stock in the bottom of a steamer (see page 143). Season with salt and saffron. Combine well. Bring to the boil and boil for 5 minutes. Add the contents of the blender. Bring to the boil again, then lower the flame.

Place those fish with the hardest flesh in the top half of the steamer. Steam for 10 minutes. Add the remaining fish and steam an additional 10 minutes.

Rub the toasted bread with the remaining garlic. Place slices of toast in the bottoms of 8 individual soup bowls. Ladle in the fish broth. Pass the fish pieces and potatoes in a separate bowl.

Serves: 8

Tomato Soup, Italian Style

8 ripe tomatoes, diced	2 tablespoons parsley, chopped
½ pound (250 grams) scallions (shallots), finely chopped	1 teaspoon lemon juice
	1 teaspoon salt
2 cloves garlic, crushed	½ teaspoon black pepper
1 stalk celery, grated	A pinch of sugar
1 tablespoon green pepper, finely diced	1 tablespoon margarine
	1 tablespoon flour
½ teaspoon oregano	2 tablespoons cream
2 tablespoons oil	Croutons
2 bay leaves	1 hard-cooked egg, mashed

Cook the tomatoes, scallions, garlic, celery, oregano and green pepper in oil for 15 minutes. After 5 minutes, add the bay leaves and parsley. Put the cooked vegetables through a food mill. Season with lemon juice, salt, pepper and sugar.

Melt the margarine in a saucepan. Stir in the flour, mixing well. Add the cream, stirring constantly until the mixture thickens. Blend the thickening into a tomato soup and cook over a low flame, stirring occasionally, for a few minutes.

Sprinkle with croutons and mashed, hard-cooked egg and serve at once.

Serves: 6

Spicy Fruit and Vegetable Soup

2 cups grapes	1 cup water
3 pounds (1½ kilograms) ripe tomatoes, sliced	2 teaspoons salt
2 firm apples, sliced	1 tablespoon lemon juice, sweetened
2 scallions (shallots), sliced	1 teaspoon sugar
1 carrot, peeled and sliced	2 egg yolks, beaten
1 stalk celery, chopped	1 cup sour cream
1 green pepper, seeded and diced	1 tablespoon cumin

Cut the grapes in half.

Place the tomatoes, apples, scallions, carrot, celery, pepper and grapes in a soup pot with 1 cup water. Season with 1 teaspoon salt. Simmer for 15 minutes. Bring the mixture to the boil, lower the flame and cook an additional 45 minutes. Remove from the flame. Cool. Force through a large strainer. Add the remaining salt, the lemon juice and the sugar.

Place the beaten egg yolks and the sour cream in a mixing bowl. Stir in some of the strained soup and blend thoroughly. Return the egg yolk or sour cream mixture to the remaining soup, mixing well. Sprinkle with cumin.

Serve hot or cold.

Serves: 6

Grape Soup

3 cups water
1 cup grapefruit juice
½ cup dry white wine
½ cup sugar
½ teaspoon cinnamon
2 cloves

1 tablespoon mint leaves, chopped
1 cup cornstarch
1 egg yolk
2 cups white grapes

Bring the water, grapefruit juice, wine, sugar, spices and mint leaves to the boil. Thicken with cornstarch. Remove from the flame.

Stir in the egg yolk, blending thoroughly. Add the grapes.

Chill well before serving.

Serves: 6

Potato Soup

2½ cups potatoes, peeled and diced
4 cups water
2 cups chicken stock
6 cloves garlic
1 teaspoon coarse (kosher) salt
¼ cup of oil

1 stalk celery, finely chopped
2 scallions (shallots), minced
1 tablespoon mint leaves, chopped
Lemon juice to taste
Pinch of cayenne pepper
Chopped parsley

Boil the potatoes until tender in water and chicken stock.

Crush the garlic with 1 teaspoon salt. Heat the oil to the smoking point and add the salted garlic. Cook for a moment then combine with the potato soup. Stir in the celery, scallions, mint leaves and lemon juice. Season with cayenne pepper. Simmer over a low flame for 10 minutes.

Sprinkle with chopped parsley and serve at once.

Serves: 6

Mushroom Soup

1 pound (500 grams) mushrooms, sliced
2 tablespoons margarine
1 teaspoon paprika
½ teaspoon oregano
2 tablespoons flour
½ teaspoon salt

¼ teaspoon black pepper
8 cups chicken stock
3 tablespoons dry sherry
1 egg yolk
2 cups sour cream
1 tablespoon chives, chopped

Sauté the mushrooms in margarine over a low flame for 3 minutes. Add the paprika and cook an additional 3 minutes.

Stir in the paprika, oregano, flour, salt, pepper, chicken stock and sherry. Cook over a low flame for 45 minutes, stirring from time to time.

Put the egg yolk in the bottom of a soup tureen. Add the sour cream and blend thoroughly. Pour in the prepared soup, sprinkle with chives and serve at once.

Serves: 8

Pomegranate and Chicken Soup

1 pound (500 grams) chicken, boned and diced
¼ cup celery, diced
4 scallions, peeled and halved
5 cups water

1 eggplant, peeled and cut into 1-inch-long strips
2 pomegranates
¼ cup sugar
½ teaspoon salt
Juice of ½ lime

Cook the chicken, celery and scallions in 5 cups boiling water for 20 minutes. Add the eggplant and continue cooking for an additional 15 minutes.

While the soup is cooking, cut the pomegranates in half and scoop out the seeds. Put the seeds in a blender and blend thoroughly. Strain the resulting mixture. Add the pomegranate juice to the soup.

Season with sugar, salt and lime juice. Simmer for an additional 20 minutes. Serve hot.

Serves: 4

Beet Soup with Cucumbers

2 medium beets, boiled, skinned and diced	2 teaspoons chives, chopped
	Salt and black pepper to taste
½ cup beet leaves, washed and chopped	4 potatoes, peeled and thickly sliced
4 cups sour milk	Chicken stock
4 cups sour cream	2 cups cucumber, chopped
1 tablespoon scallion, minced	4 hard-cooked eggs, sliced

Combine the beets, beet leaves, milk, sour cream, scallion and chives. Blend thoroughly. Season with salt and pepper. Place in a saucepan and bring to the boil. Boil for 5 minutes. Cool. Refrigerate for at least 2 hours.

Boil the potatoes in chicken stock until tender. Keep warm.

Cover the cucumbers with boiling water for 3 minutes, rinse in cold water and drain. Stir the cucumbers and eggs into the beet mixture.

Place the hot potato slices in the bottoms of 6 individual soup bowls. Add the beet soup. Serve at once.

Serves: 6

CHICKEN
and
TURKEY

Chicken in Wine

A 2½-pound (1.2 kilogram) broiling chicken
4 tablespoons oil
3 sliced tomatoes
7 cloves garlic, finely chopped
½ cup cognac
2½ cups dry white wine
2 stalks celery with their leaves, cut in two
2 stalks fennel, cut in two
15 green olives
1 teaspoon salt
¼ teaspoon black pepper
4 bay leaves
¼ teaspoon thyme
Pinch of ginger
2 unpeeled, sliced oranges (optional)

Cut the chicken into parts and pan-broil well on all sides in oil. Add sliced tomatoes and half of the garlic. Reduce heat. When chicken begins to brown, stir in the cognac, wine, celery, fennel, olives and the remaining garlic. Season with salt, pepper, bay leaves, thyme and ginger. Continue cooking over a low flame for 20-30 minutes. When chicken is tender, add sliced oranges and leave on flame a few minutes more.

Accompany with Spanish rice (see below) and garnish with additional orange slices (optional).

Serves: 4

Spanish Rice

4 cups chicken broth
⅔ cup oil
2 teaspoons salt
2 cups rice
1 small can sliced mushrooms, drained
1 tablespoon margarine
1 tablespoon parsley, chopped

Bring the chicken broth, oil and salt to a boil. Add the rice. Cook over a medium flame until all liquid is absorbed. If rice is not yet soft, add water and boil for a few minutes more. Remove from flame. Cover pot tightly and drape with a tea towel. Let sit for 10 minutes. Heat mushrooms in margarine, stir into rice, sprinkle with parsley and serve at once.

Serves: 8

Roast Stuffed Chicken in Pomegranate Sauce

A 2-pound (1-kilogram) roasting chicken
½ lemon
5 scallions (shallots), chopped
3 tablespoons oil
1 cup lean beef, finely diced
½ cup water

1 tablespoon parsley, chopped
½ teaspoon salt
¼ teaspoon black pepper
½ teaspoon cinnamon
Juice of 1 pomegranate
1 tablespoon sugar
3 tablespoons lemon juice
1 stick (125 grams) margarine

Rinse and salt the chicken. Rub it with lemon. Set aside. Sauté the scallions in oil. Add the meat and stir in ½ cup cold water. Continue cooking until the water evaporates, stirring from time to time. Place on paper towels to drain off the oil, return to pan and add parsley, salt, pepper, cinnamon, pomegranate juice, sugar and lemon juice. Blend thoroughly.

Stuff the chicken with the prepared stuffing and place it in a roasting pan, greased with margarine. Coat the chicken breasts and wings with the remaining margarine. Roast in a medium oven (350°) for ½ hour. Reduce heat to 300° and cook for an additional 3 hours.

Serves: 4

Chicken and Vegetable Stew

1 cup chick peas
¼ teaspoon baking soda
4 scallions (shallots), chopped
A 5-pound (2½-kilogram) stew-
    ing chicken, cut into parts
2 pounds (1 kilogram) fresh
    spinach, rinsed and chopped

1 onion, chopped and sautéed
    in oil
4 stalks celery, chopped
½ teaspoon salt
¼ teaspoon black pepper
Chicken stock

Soak the chick peas and soda overnight in water to cover. Rinse and drain.

Place the scallions, the chicken parts, ½ the chick peas, ½ the spinach, the fried onion, the celery, the remaining chick peas and the rest of the spinach in a flameproof casserole. Season with salt and pepper and cook over a medium flame for 10 minutes. Add enough chicken stock to cover and continue cooking over a low flame for 2-3 hours.

Serves: 8

Chicken Pie with Walnuts

A 2-pound (1-kilogram) roasting
    chicken, boned and cut into
    small pieces
1 onion
2 stalks celery with leaves
1 carrot
4 cups water

1 teaspoon salt
½ teaspoon black pepper
2 cups walnuts, shelled
5 eggs, beaten
2 tablespoons parsley, chopped
4 cloves garlic, crushed
Pinch of ginger

Place the chicken pieces in a large pot with the onion, celery and carrot. Add the water, salt and pepper. Stew until only about 1½ cups water remain in the pot. Discard the vegetables.

Crush the walnuts. Mix well with the eggs, parsley, garlic and ginger.

Drain the chicken thoroughly and place in a baking dish. Cover with the nut mixture and bake in a medium oven (350°) for ½ hour. Serve with a mixed vegetable salad.

Serves: 6

Chicken in Apple and Brandy Sauce

2 young chickens, quartered	½ teaspoon salt
2 sticks (250 grams) margarine	¼ teaspoon black pepper
¼ cup brandy	½ teaspoon cinnamon
6 apples, peeled, cored and cubed	1 clove
	1 cup apple juice
2 onions, chopped	½ pound (250 grams) fresh
1 tablespoon parsley, chopped	mushrooms, finely sliced

Brown the chicken pieces in a frying pan in ½ the margarine. Cover with the brandy and ignite. Shake the pot until the alcohol is burned off. Set aside.

In a second frying pan, melt the remaining margarine and cook the apples until tender. Add the onions and parsley and simmer 5 minutes.

Transfer the chicken, apples and onions to a flameproof casserole. Add the salt, pepper, cinnamon, clove and apple juice. Cover and cook over a medium flame for 45 minutes. Add the mushrooms and cook 15 minutes more.

Serves: 6

Curried Chicken in Wine

6 chicken quarters	¾ cup oil
1 teaspoon salt	1 pound (500 grams) scallions
½ teaspoon black pepper	(shallots), chopped
½ teaspoon curry powder	1 cup dry white wine
1 cup flour	¼ cup parsley, chopped

Dip the chicken quarters into a mixture of salt, pepper and curry. Dip in flour and fry in oil. Remove the chicken and reserve.

Sauté the scallions in the oil remaining in the pan. Add the wine and chicken. Sprinkle with parsley. Cook over a low flame until the chicken has absorbed all the wine.

Serves: 6

Chicken with Lima Beans and Mushrooms

2 scallions, chopped	3 tablespoons water
1 stick (125 grams) margarine	½ tablespoon salt
2 pounds (1 kilogram) fresh	A 2-pound (1-kilogram) chicken
lima beans	1 small can mushrooms,
2 tablespoons green pepper,	drained
diced	

Sauté the scallions in margarine until golden. Add the lima beans and green pepper. Sauté 2-3 minutes. Add 3 tablespoons water and the salt. Cover tightly and cook over a low flame for ½ hour, stirring occasionally.

Divide the chicken into pieces and add to the lima bean mixture. Cover tightly and cook for 1 hour, or until the chicken and lima beans are very tender. Stir every 20 minutes, adding water if needed. Immediately before serving, heat the mushrooms and add them to the dish.

Serves: 4

Chicken with Apple Casserole

6 chicken quarters	½ cup apple juice
5 ounces (150 grams) canned	1 clove
apples, drained	½ teaspoon salt
½ cup oil	¼ teaspoon black pepper
4 scallions (shallots), chopped	½ teaspoon cinnamon

Brown the chicken quarters and the apples in oil in a flameproof casserole. Remove from casserole and reserve. Add the scallions to the casserole and sauté until golden. Stir in the apple juice. Return the chicken to the casserole and season with the clove, salt, pepper and cinnamon.

Cover and cook over a low heat for 1 hour. After 45 minutes add the apples.

Serves: 6

Chicken in Pineapple and Cherry Sauce

6 chicken quarters	½ cup wine vinegar
½ teaspoon ginger, ground	Soy sauce
1 cup flour	1 small can pineapple chunks,
2 sticks (250 grams) margarine	undrained
2 cups chicken stock	1 small can red cherries
1 cup brown sugar	

Split the chicken quarters in half. Rinse and dry well. Sprinkle with ginger, dip in flour and brown in margarine in a flameproof casserole.

Combine the stock, sugar and vinegar in a saucepan. Add soy sauce according to taste. Pour the resulting mixture over the chicken.

Add the pineapple, with its syrup, and the cherries. Cook over a medium flame for ½ hour.

Serves: 6

Sweet and Sour Chicken

3 tablespoons currants
⅔ cup beef, ground
1 egg
½ slice white bread, soaked in water and squeezed dry
1 teaspoon parsley, chopped
¾ teaspoon salt
⅛ teaspoon black pepper
3 scallions (shallots), chopped
2 pounds (1 kilogram) chicken pieces

3 cups water
¼ pound (125 grams) lean beef, diced
½ cup dry red wine
1 tablespoon honey
Juice of ½ lemon
4 teaspoons sugar
1 teaspoon brown sugar
1 egg, separated
1 tablespoon semolina
Oil for frying

Soak the currants in water for 20 minutes.

Combine the ground meat, egg, bread, parsley, ½ teaspoon salt and black pepper, blending well. Form into small meatballs. Reserve. Brown the scallions and chicken lightly in oil before putting them into a flameproof casserole dish. Add the water, diced beef and the reserved meatballs, cover and cook for ½ hour. After ½ hour incorporate the currants, wine, honey, lemon juice, 3 teaspoons sugar and the brown sugar. Continue cooking until chicken is tender.

Beat the egg white until foamy with the remaining sugar. Add the yolk, the semolina and the remaining salt and shape into small balls. Sauté the prepared balls in hot oil and add them to the chicken mixture. Simmer for an additional 10 minutes.

Serves: 6

Lemon-flavored Chicken

2 pounds (1 kilogram) chicken wings and drumsticks
2 cups pure lemon juice
1 teaspoon salt

½ teaspoon black pepper
Margarine
Lemon slices
Gherkins

Marinate the chicken in lemon juice, salt and pepper for at least 24 hours in the refrigerator, turning the chicken pieces from time to time. Remove from the marinade and dry thoroughly. Rub with margarine.

Place the chicken pieces under the broiler (grill) for 15-20 minutes. Garnish with lemon slices and gherkins.

Serves: 6

Braised Chicken with Wine and Mushrooms

2 young chickens
½ cup oil
2 onions, sliced
2 scallions (shallots), sliced
2 green peppers, seeded and diced
2 pimientos, sliced
1 stalk celery, chopped

2 cloves garlic, chopped
1 teaspoon salt
1 teaspoon black pepper
1 cup chicken stock
½ cup sweet red wine
1 small can sliced mushrooms, drained

Bone and chunk the chicken. Fry in oil until brown. Add the sliced vegetables and garlic. Season with salt and pepper. Moisten with chicken stock and red wine. Cover and cook over a low flame until the chicken is tender. Stir occasionally. Before serving, add the mushrooms and heat them through. Accompany with rice or noodles.

Serves: 8

Baked Stuffed Chicken

A 4-pound (2-kilogram) roasting chicken
1 teaspoon salt
½ teaspoon black pepper
1 teaspoon mustard
1 onion, minced
Pinch of cayenne pepper
2 cloves garlic, crushed
⅓ cup rice

½ cup lean meat, ground
1 tomato, chopped
2 teaspoons green olives, chopped
2 ounces (60 grams) margarine, in bits
1 tablespoon oil
1 onion, sliced

Coat the chicken, inside and out, with a mixture of ½ teaspoon salt, the pepper, mustard, onion, cayenne pepper and garlic.

Mix the rice in with the meat, tomato, olives, remaining salt and margarine bits. Stuff the chicken with the resulting mixture. Sew the opening closed and place the stuffed chicken in a pan greased with 1 tablespoon oil. Place the sliced onion around the chicken and bake in a hot oven (400°) for 1½ hours, basting from time to time with the pan juices.

Serves: 6

Stuffed Chicken with Cauliflower

A 1½-pound (750-gram) frying chicken
½ pound (250 grams) lean beef, ground
2 teaspoons parsley, finely chopped
1 clove garlic, crushed
1 teaspoon onion, minced
1 teaspoon Worcestershire sauce
2 eggs, 1 of them beaten
½ teaspoon salt
¼ teaspoon black pepper
½ teaspoon paprika
1 cup oil
A 1-pound (500-gram) cauliflower
4 tablespoons water

Divide the chicken into 6 portions.

Combine the meat, parsley, garlic, onion, Worcestershire sauce and whole egg. Mix well. Season with salt, pepper and paprika.

Make a slit in each of the chicken pieces and stuff with some of the meat mixture. Dip the stuffed chicken in beaten egg and fry in ⅓ of the oil on the slit side. Reserve.

Divide the cauliflower into 6 portions. Boil in salted water to cover for 5 minutes. Drain and dry the cauliflower and coat each cauliflower piece with a thin layer of meat, dip in beaten egg and sauté in ⅓ cup oil.

Place the stuffed chicken in a flameproof casserole with the remaining oil. Add the cauliflower and 4 tablespoons water. Cover. Bring to the boil, lower the flame and cook for ½ hour.

Serves: 6

Baked Chicken and Bananas

6 chicken breasts, boned and pounded thin
1 teaspoon salt
½ teaspoon black pepper

6 bananas, peeled and mashed
1 teaspoon brown sugar
3 cups salted peanuts, crushed
Oil for frying

Salt the chicken on both sides and pepper one side.

Combine the mashed banana, brown sugar and peanuts. Spread the resulting mixture over the chicken breasts, roll them up and tie them with string. Sauté the stuffed breasts in oil on all sides. Reserve. Prepare the sauce.

Sauce

1 small carrot, grated
¼ pound (125 grams) olives, pitted and ground
2 egg yolks, hard-cooked and mashed
½ teaspoon salt
½ teaspoon paprika

1 tablespoon chives, finely chopped
2 ounces (60 grams) margarine
½ cup flour
2 cups chicken stock
¼ cup dry white wine

Combine the carrot, olives and egg yolks and blend thoroughly. Mix in the salt, paprika and chives.

Melt the margarine in a saucepan, stir in the flour, blending well, and add the chicken stock and wine. Bring to the boil, stirring constantly. Remove from the flame. Cool.

Add the carrot mixture to the prepared sauce, mixing well. Place the chicken breasts in a baking dish, pour in any oil remaining in the sautéeing pan, cover with prepared sauce and bake in a medium oven (350°) for ½ hour.

Serves: 6

Chicken Rolls in Wine Sauce

1 carrot, grated
¼ cup green peas
1 stalk celery, finely diced
2 tomatoes, peeled and chopped
2 tablespoons cucumber pickle, diced

1 tablespoon parsley, finely chopped
6 chicken breasts, boned and pounded thin
1 cup dry white wine

Combine the carrot, peas, celery, tomatoes and pickle. Mix in the parsley. Spread the vegetable mixture over the flattened chicken breasts. Roll closed and secure with toothpicks. Simmer in wine for ½ hour. Serve as an appetizer.

Serves: 6

Chicken in Barbecue Sauce

2 roasting chickens, quartered
Mustard
1 teaspoon salt

1 teaspoon paprika
Margarine

Prepare the sauce (see below).

Rub the chicken quarters with mustard. Sprinkle with salt and paprika and brown in margarine.

Place in a baking pan and add the prepared sauce. Bake in a medium oven (350°) for 1 hour, basting with the pan juices from time to time.

Sauce

1 cup coffee
½ cup tomato ketchup
½ cup wine vinegar
2 cloves garlic, crushed
¼ cup soy sauce

Pinch of hot pepper
½ cup brown sugar
2 ounces (60 grams) margarine
Juice of ½ lime

Place all the above ingredients in a large saucepan and bring to the boil. Boil for 5 minutes, stirring constantly. Set aside to cool, then refrigerate.

Serves: 8

Chicken in Honey and Orange Juice

A 4-5 pound (2-2½-kilogram) roasting chicken
1 teaspoon salt
5 teaspoons chicken fat or margarine
¼ cup honey
1 teaspoon paprika

2 scallions (shallots), sliced
1 tablespoon green pepper, diced
1 cup orange juice
Orange slices
Parsley sprigs

Salt the chicken and let it stand for a few minutes. Meanwhile melt the chicken fat or margarine and combine it with the honey. Coat the chicken inside and out with this mixture. Sprinkle with paprika.

Put the sliced scallions and green pepper in a deep baking dish. Cover with a piece of muslin and place the chicken on top. Heat the orange juice and pour over the chicken.

Bake in a hot oven (400°) until brown. Lower the heat to 350° and continue to bake until the chicken is tender. Baste the chicken from time to time with the pan liquids and turn it occasionally. Remove from the oven and garnish with orange slices and parsley sprigs.

Serve with an orange sauce.

Serves: 6

Chicken and Scallions, Yemenite Style

2 scallions (shallots), chopped
6 tablespoons oil
6 chicken quarters
1 teaspoon salt

1 tablespoon mixed spices: black pepper, cumin, ginger, cloves, saffron
1 cup chicken stock

Sauté the scallions in oil in a flameproof casserole. Add the chicken and brown. Incorporate the salt, spices and chicken stock. Cover and cook over a low flame until the chicken is tender (about 1 hour). Add more stock if necessary.

Serves: 6

Chicken Canapés with Quince

3 quinces	1 clove
1 cup orange juice	¼ teaspoon ginger
¼ cup dry white wine	Salt and black pepper to taste

Peel the quinces and cut them into strips. Place the quince strips in a marinade of orange juice, wine and the spices. Refrigerate for 3 hours. Prepare the canapés.

Canapés

1¼ pounds (625 grams) chicken, boned	¼ teaspoon ginger
	¼ teaspoon cinnamon
4 scallions (shallots), chopped and sautéed	Chopped parsley
	Salt and black pepper to taste
1 carrot, sliced and cooked	2 eggs
4 stalks celery, chopped and cooked	6 tablespoons bread crumbs
	4 tablespoons oil

Put the chicken and vegetables through the grinder. Add the ginger, cinnamon, parsley, salt and pepper. Combine well.

Incorporate the eggs and 4 tablespoons bread crumbs and work the resulting mixture into a dough. Roll out the dough and divide it into 16 triangles. Arrange the triangles in a large baking tin greased with 4 tablespoons oil and sprinkled with 2 tablespoons crumbs. Prepare the filling.

Filling

½ pound (250 grams) chicken livers, chopped and sautéed	3 stalks celery, chopped
	1 tablespoon bread crumbs
2 scallions (shallots), chopped and sautéed	1 tablespoon canned mushrooms, drained and chopped

Combine the above ingredients and blend thoroughly. Mound onto the prepared pastry triangles.

To assemble

Lettuce leaves

Drain the marinated quince strips, reserving the marinade, and place them in the baking tin with the filled triangles. Bake in a hot oven (400°) for 20 minutes. Remove from the oven and pour in the reserved marinade. Stir in the sauce (see below) and return the tin to the oven for a few minutes. Serve the canapés on a bed of lettuce garnished with quince strips.

Sauce

3 tablespoons bread crumbs	2 egg yolks, beaten
3 tablespoons oil	2 teaspoons lime juice
2 cups chicken stock, boiling	Salt and black pepper to taste

Heat the oil in a saucepan and add the bread crumbs. Stir until the crumbs are golden. Add the chicken stock and egg yolks, stirring constantly. Remove from the flame and season with lime juice, salt and pepper.

Chicken and Pecan Doughnuts

½ cup pecans
2 scallions (shallots), chopped
Oil for deep-frying
1 teaspoon salt
¼ teaspoon black pepper
1 tablespoon parsley, chopped

2 tablespoons raisins, chopped
2 gherkins, chopped
½ pound (250 grams) chicken breast
1 pound (500 grams) yeast dough

Blanch the pecans in boiling water for 3 minutes. Remove the outer skins and chop the nutmeats.

Sauté the scallions in oil. Add ½ teaspoon salt, the pepper, parsley and pecans. Cook for a few minutes then stir in the raisins and gherkins. Combine well. Remove from flame.

Cook the chicken in boiling water for 5 minutes. Drain, bone and dice. Sauté the diced chicken in oil until brown, with the remaining salt. Be sure that the chicken does not become dry. Drain the oil from the chicken and add the chicken pieces to the mixture.

Divide the dough into 6 parts. Roll out each piece into a rectangle and fill with the chicken mixture. Roll closed and connect the open ends to form a ring. The rings may be deep-fried in oil or baked in a medium oven (350°) until done.

Serves: 6

Sautéed Chicken with Pomegranates

A 2-pound (1 kilogram) young chicken
4 tablespoons oil
2 scallions (shallots), sliced

2 pomegranates
3 cloves garlic, crushed
1 teaspoon salt
¼ cup pine nuts

Cut the chicken into pieces. Sauté in oil with the sliced scallion until brown (about ½ hour).

Peel the pomegranates, chop coarsely and add to the pan along with the garlic. Season with salt. Cook for about 15 minutes, stirring from time to time. Stir in the pine nuts and serve at once.

Serves: 4

Curried Chicken Pot Pie

Yeast dough
2 pounds (1 kilogram) chicken, cooked
1 can cream of mushroom soup, condensed
2 tablespoons parsley, chopped
3 pimientos, chopped
1 teaspoon curry powder
1 teaspoon salt
½ teaspoon black pepper
Chicken stock
1 egg yolk, diluted in 1 tablespoon milk

Roll out the dough. Use about ½ to line a glass pie dish. Reserve the rest. Dice the chicken and combine it with the mushroom soup, parsley, pimientos, curry powder, salt and pepper. Thin with chicken stock if necessary.

Fill the pie shell with the above mixture and cover with the reserved dough, sealing the edges closed. Prick the pie-crust cover in several places with a fork and coat it with egg yolk.

Bake in a hot oven (400°) for 45 minutes.

Serves: 6

Chicken and Walnut Balls

½ pound (250 grams) chicken breasts, boned
¼ cup walnuts
2 onions
Oil for frying
2 scallions (shallots)
3 carrots, sliced
1 stalk celery, chopped
1 teaspoon salt
½ teaspoon black pepper
½ teaspoon sugar
3 cups chicken stock
1 egg
1 tablespoon flour

Put the chicken, walnuts and 1 onion through the grinder. Chop and sauté the remaining onion in oil and add to the chicken mixture. Reserve.

Slice the scallions and put them in a saucepan with the carrots and celery. Season with ½ teaspoon salt, ¼ teaspoon black pepper and sugar. Add the chicken stock and bring to the boil. Cook for 15 minutes.

Add the egg and flour to the chicken mixture. Season with the remaining salt and pepper. Combine well. Shape into balls and add to the cooked vegetables. Cook over a medium flame for ½ hour. Serve hot.

Serves: 2

Stuffed Fried Chicken

½ cup plus 1 tablespoon strong chicken stock	Oil for frying
	6 chicken breasts
3 eggs, 1 of them beaten	1 teaspoon paprika
1 teaspoon parsley	6 stuffed olives
1 teaspoon salt	Flour
½ teaspoon black pepper	1 teaspoon lemon juice
Pinch of ginger	1 tablespoon oil
2 slices white bread	Bread crumbs

Combine ½ cup chicken stock with 1 beaten egg. Add ½ teaspoon parsley, ½ teaspoon salt, ¼ teaspoon pepper and the ginger. Mix thoroughly. Soak the 2 slices bread in the above mixture until they absorb all the liquid. Sauté the soaked bread in oil, on both sides, until brown then slice each piece of bread into 3 strips. Reserve.

Make a slit in the outer side of each chicken breast. Sprinkle with the remaining salt, pepper and the paprika. Stuff a strip of bread and an olive, sliced in 3, into each slit, and tie closed with kitchen string. Roll the stuffed breasts gently in flour.

Beat the 2 remaining eggs and combine them with the remaining tablespoon of chicken stock, the lemon juice, and the oil. Dip the chicken breasts in this mixture, then coat them with bread crumbs. Fry in hot oil over a low flame until tender. Remove the string and serve at once.

Serves: 6

Deep-dish Chicken in "Tangerine Champagne" Sauce

1 pound (500 grams) chicken breasts, boned
1 medium potato, peeled
1 green pepper, seeded
1 firm apple, peeled
1 carrot, peeled
8 dates, pitted
6 cloves garlic
4 eggs, separated
2 tablespoons cornstarch
2 ounces (60 grams) pistachios

1 tablespoon parsley, chopped
2½ teaspoons salt
½ teaspoon ginger
1 tablespoon margarine, softened
1½ cups "tangerine champagne" (see below)
2 tablespoons lime juice
3 scallions (shallots), finely sliced
3 pimientos, cut into strips

Put the chicken, potato, green pepper, apple, carrot, dates and garlic through the grinder. Add the egg yolks, cornstarch, pistachios, parsley, 2 teaspoons salt, ginger, margarine and "tangerine champagne". Combine well. Put the resulting mixture into a greased baking dish and bake on the upper shelf of a medium oven (350°) for 45 minutes.

While the chicken mixture is baking, whip the egg whites until stiff. Add the lime juice, remaining salt and scallions. 10 minutes before the end of the baking time, cover the chicken mixture with egg white, garnish with pimiento strips and transfer the baking dish to a lower shelf in the oven.

"Tangerine Champagne"

Tangerines   Sugar

Squeeze the tangerines and strain the juice. Place in a large glass jar.

For every 2½ cups of juice add 1 cup sugar. Seal with paraffin. Shake well. Allow to ferment for about 6 weeks.

At the end of the fermentation period, unseal the jar and strain the juice through a muslin cloth once a day for 3 days. Transfer to a bottle and store in a cool place.

The "champagne" may be kept for years.

Serves: 4

*Tehina** and Chicken Liver Canapés

1 tablespoon pine nuts	1 teaspoon salt
3 tablespoons oil	½ teaspoon ginger
1 pound (500 grams) yeast dough	½ teaspoon cinnamon
2 scallions (shallots)	1 tablespoon canned mushrooms, drained and minced
Chicken fat	½ cup prepared *tehina* (for preparation see page 20)
2 chicken gizzards	
2 chicken livers	½ cup pomegranate seeds

Toss the pine nuts in hot oil in a frying pan. Drain and reserve.

Roll out the dough to thickness of 1½ inches. Cut into 2-inch-wide circles. Place the rounds of dough on a greased baking sheet.

Chop the scallions and sauté in the oil remaining in the frying pan and the chicken fat. Chop the gizzards, dice the livers coarsely and add to the pan. Sauté the remaining mixture for 10 minutes. Season with salt, ginger and cinnamon and stir in the sautéed pine nuts and mushrooms.

Spread each circle of prepared dough with ½ teaspoon *tehina*. Top with a layer of the scallion-liver mixture. Sprinkle with pomegranate seeds. Bake in a hot oven (400°) for 10-15 minutes. Serve hot.

Serves: 4

*See page 20.

Chicken Cups

2 sticks (250 grams) margarine   ½ teaspoon salt
2½ cups flour   3 tablespoons cold water

Cut the margarine into small pieces and work into the flour. Add the salt and water and form into a dough. Refrigerate to chill. Roll out and use to line individual baking dishes. Place the baking dishes in the oven and bake at 350° until the pastry shells are golden. Set aside to cool.

Filling

2 cups chicken, cooked, boned and diced   2 pimientos, sliced
½ cup rice, boiled   ¼ teaspoon curry
2 cucumber pickles, diced   Lemon juice
¼ cup carrots, cooked and diced   Salt and black pepper to taste
1 tablespoon pine nuts   Black olives
    Mayonnaise
    Paprika

Combine the chicken, rice, pickles, carrots, pine nuts and pimientos. Blend well. Stir in the curry, moisten with lemon juice and add salt and black pepper to taste. Refrigerate.

To serve, spoon the chicken mixture into the pastry cups, garnish with black olives and dabs of mayonnaise and sprinkle with paprika.

Serves: 4

Smothered Chicken with Corn and Olives

A 3-pound (1½-kilogram)
roasting chicken
Oil for frying
1 onion, chopped
2 scallions (shallots), chopped
2 cloves
2 tablespoons flour
4 cups hot chicken stock
2 tablespoons parsley, chopped

¼ teaspoon thyme
1 teaspoon salt
½ teaspoon black pepper
4 bay leaves
2 eggs, beaten
5 cups canned corned kernels, drained
¼ cup stuffed green olives, sliced

Divide the chicken into portions and brown in oil in a flameproof casserole. Remove and reserve. Sauté the onion, scallions and cloves together in the oil remaining in the casserole. Sprinkle the onion and scallions with flour and add the chicken stock.

Bring to the boil, stirring constantly, and add the parsley, thyme, salt, pepper, bay leaves and reserved chicken. Bring to the boil again. Lower the flame and cook for 45 minutes, or until the chicken is tender.

Stir in the beaten eggs and the corn. Continue cooking an additional ½ hour. 5 minutes before the dish is done, stir in the olives.

Serves: 6

Honeyed Chicken Balls with Rum

1½ pounds (750 grams) chicken, boned
1 cup bread crumbs
1 teaspoon sugar
1 teaspoon flour
1 egg
2 teaspoons parsley, chopped
½ teaspoon salt
¼ teaspoon black pepper
¼ teaspoon cinnamon
A grating of lemon rind

Put the chicken and bread crumbs through the grinder. Add the remaining ingredients, combine thoroughly and form into balls. Cook the chicken balls in sauce.

Sauce

2 scallions (shallots), chopped
1 tablespoon oil
½ cup water
2 tablespoons honey
Juice of 1 lemon
1 tablespoon sugar
1 tablespoon rum

Sauté the scallions in oil. Add ½ cup water, the honey and the lemon juice. Bring to the boil, stirring constantly. When the mixture boils, add the patties to the pan. Cover with water and simmer for 20 minutes on low flame.

While the mixture is simmering, brown the sugar, thin with a little water and add to the sauce.

Serves: 4

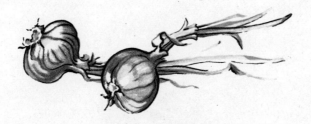

Chicken and Asparagus Salad

2 pounds (1 kilogram)
asparagus, cooked and drained
French dressing (see below)
1 cup mayonnaise
1 clove garlic, crushed
2 teaspoons lemon juice
⅛ teaspoon saffron
4 tablespoons onion, minced
4 cups chicken, cooked and diced

1 cup celery, chopped
4 hard-cooked eggs, sliced
1 tablespoon green olives,
 pitted (stoned) and chopped
1 teaspoon capers
Salt and black pepper to taste
Lettuce leaves
1 tablespoon parsley, chopped

Trim and dice the asparagus and marinate in French dressing to cover for 2 hours. Drain.

Combine the mayonnaise, garlic, lemon juice, saffron and onion. Moisten with French dressing. Combine well.

Place the chicken, asparagus, celery, eggs, olives and capers in a mixing bowl. Add the seasoned mayonnaise and mix well. Salt and pepper to taste. Refrigerate. Mound onto a bed of lettuce, sprinkle with parsley and serve at once.

French dressing

½ teaspoon mustard
6 tablespoons olive oil
2 tablespoons vinegar
1 teaspoon sugar

1 clove garlic, crushed
Salt and black pepper to taste
Paprika
1 teaspoon honey

Incorporate the mustard into the olive oil. Place in a glass jar. Add the remaining ingredients, seal the jar and shake well.

Serves: 6

Chicken and *Tehina** Pie

3 chicken breasts, boned
1 small can sliced mushrooms,
drained
¼ teaspoon thyme

2 tablespoons orange brandy
Tehina (for preparation see
below)
Lettuce leaves

Put the chicken through the grinder. Add the mushrooms, thyme, brandy and 4 tablespoons prepared *tehina*.

Line a greased pie plate with ¾ of the remaining *tehina*. Cover with the chicken mixture and top with the remaining *tehina*. Bake in a medium oven (350°) for 40 minutes.

Serve with a cold salad.

To prepare *tehina*

1 cup water
Juice of 1 lemon
Juice of 3 tangerines
½ pound (250 grams) semi-
prepared *tehina*

8 cloves garlic, crushed
2 tablespoons parsley,
chopped
1 teaspoon salt

Blend the water, lemon juice and tangerine juice into the semi-prepared *tehina*. Stir in the garlic, parsley and salt. Combine well.

Serves: 4

* See page 20.

Red Wine Chicken Kebabs

6 chicken breasts, boned
Juice of 5 lemons
1½ cups oil
2 cups dry red wine
3 garlic cloves, minced
3 bay leaves
1 teaspoon salt
½ teaspoon black pepper

3 green peppers, seeded and
cut into 12 1½-inch squares
3 celery stalks, sliced
3 onions, quartered
6 large mushrooms, washed
and trimmed
Melted margarine

Cut the chicken breasts into 1½-inch cubes.

Prepare a marinade of lemon juice, oil, red wine, garlic, bay leaves, salt and pepper. Soak the chicken pieces in this mixture overnight. Drain and dry thoroughly.

Alternate pieces of chicken, pepper, celery and onion on 6 skewers. Finish each skewer with a large mushroom.

Brush the meat and vegetables with melted margarine and grill for 15 minutes.

Serves: 6

Chicken and Potato Pie

3 medium potatoes
6 eggs
2 eggs, hard-cooked
3 pimientos, chopped
¼ cup canned mushrooms,
drained and sliced

1 tablespoon salt
¼ teaspoon black pepper
4 chicken breasts, boned,
cooked and sliced

Boil and mash the potatoes. Add the 6 eggs and combine well. Gently stir in the sliced eggs, pimientos, mushrooms, salt and pepper. Incorporate the sliced chicken.

Transfer the chicken mixture to a greased baking dish. Bake for 20 minutes in a medium oven (350°). Slice and serve.

Serves: 6

Israeli Stuffed Chicken

A 4-pound (2-kilogram) chicken, very fatty
1 pound (500 grams) chicken breast and chicken livers
2 ounces (60 grams) pine nuts
10 eggs, 3 of them hard-cooked
2 tablespoons matzo meal

¼ cup parsley, chopped
2 tablespoons onion, minced
½ teaspoon salt
¼ teaspoon black pepper
⅛ teaspoon thyme
3 grains cardamon, ground and crushed
2 cups water

Carefully skin the chicken with a sharp knife, leaving the skin intact. Reserve the whole chicken skin. Cut chicken into parts.

Put the chicken breast and livers through the grinder. Reserve the remaining chicken parts. Add the pine nuts, eggs, matzo meal, parsley and onion. Season with salt, pepper, thyme and cardamon.

Stuff the reserved chicken skin with the prepared filling. Fasten securely and cook in 2 cups boiling water for ½ hour.

Accompany with the remaining chicken pieces, stewed or roasted.

Serves: 8

Roast Chicken Stuffed with Quince, in Orange Sauce

A 4-pound (2-kilogram) roasting chicken
1 tablespoon salt
½ teaspoon paprika
¼ teaspoon tarragon

2 quinces, peeled
1 tablespoon flour
Orange slices
Black olives

Prepare the chicken for roasting. Rub the dressed bird, inside and out, with a mixture of salt, paprika and tarragon. Stuff with the whole quinces and sew the stuffed bird closed. Sprinkle with 1 tablespoon flour.

Arrange the chicken in a roasting pan. Place in a very hot oven (450°). Reduce the heat immediately to 350° and roast for 1½ hours, basting from time to time with the pan juices. When the bird is ready, transfer to a platter and spoon on the prepared sauce. Garnish with orange slices and black olives.

Sauce

1 tablespoon vinegar
¼ cup sugar
1 cup orange juice

2 tablespoons curaçao or other orange brandy
1 teaspoon lemon juice
⅛ teaspoon salt

Put the vinegar and sugar in a saucepan. Cook over a low flame until the sugar begins to brown. Add the remaining ingredients and bring to the boil.

Serves: 8

Chicken and Vegetable Casserole

4 onions, sliced into thin
rings
2 cups chicken, boned
4 medium potatoes, thinly
sliced
1 tablespoon parsley, chopped
½ teaspoon salt
1 teaspoon cumin
1 teaspoon saffron
6 cloves garlic, chopped

½ cup pumpkin, peeled and
chopped
½ cup squash, peeled and
chopped
1 small can mushrooms, drained
and chopped
4 tomatoes, peeled and sliced
½ cup oil
Chicken stock
2 teaspoons lemon juice

Line a greased baking dish with ½ the onion slices. Cover with ½ the chicken. Top the chicken with ½ the potatoes. Sprinkle with ½ the parsley. Season with ½ the salt, cumin, saffron and garlic, blended thoroughly.

Combine the squash, pumpkin and mushrooms and spread ½ the resulting mixture over the layer of seasoning. Finish with ½ the tomato slices.

Repeat the process with the remaining chicken, seasoning and vegetables, starting with a second layer of onions. Cover the final layer of tomatoes with ½ cup oil.

Bake in a medium oven (350°) for ½ hour, or until brown, adding chicken stock if the mixture appears too dry. A few minutes before removing the casserole from the oven, sprinkle with lemon juice.

Serves: 4

Chicken Liver Balls

1 large onion, sliced
3 scallions (shallots), sliced
1½ cups oil
2 chicken livers
4 slices white bread, soaked
in water and squeezed dry

1 tablespoon parsley, finely chopped
1 egg
½ teaspoon salt
¼ teaspoon black pepper
1 tablespoon matzo meal

Sauté the onion and scallions in ¼ cup oil. Add the chicken livers and fry for 5 minutes. Add the bread and continue frying an additional 5 minutes.

Put the contents of the frying pan through the grinder. Add the parsley, egg, seasonings and matzo meal. Blend thoroughly and allow to cool. Shape into balls and fry in the remaining oil.

Serves: 4

Giblets in Wine and Parsley Sauce

18-24 chicken giblets
2 tablespoons margarine
2 cloves garlic, finely chopped
2 tablespoons flour
½ cup dry white wine

½ teaspoon salt
¼ teaspoon black pepper
1 egg yolk
1 cup parsley, finely chopped
Slices of toasted bread

Clean the giblets and cook in boiling water until tender (about 1 hour). Remove to a dish and reserve the broth.

Melt the margarine in a large saucepan and sauté the garlic in it. Add the flour, wine and ½ cup of the reserved broth. Continue cooking and stirring until you obtain a thick, clear sauce. Add more broth as necessary. Season with the salt and pepper. Beat in the egg yolk and incorporate the parsley. Add the giblets to the saucepan and simmer for a few minutes more. Serve on toast.

Serves: 6

Chicken Livers with Mushrooms in Wine

¾ pound (350 grams) chicken livers, sliced
3 tablespoons oil
4 scallions (shallots), chopped
½ teaspoon salt
¼ teaspoon black pepper
1 cup chicken stock

1 tablespoon flour, mixed with a little oil
¼ pound (125 grams) mushrooms
1 cup dry white wine
½ teaspoon lemon juice
2 tablespoons parsley, chopped

Sauté the chicken livers in oil with the scallions. Add salt, pepper and chicken stock. Cook over a low flame for ½ hour, adding more stock if necessary.

Stir in the flour, mixed with a little oil, and blend thoroughly. Add the mushrooms, cut into small pieces, and the wine. Cook an additional 15 minutes. Stir in the lemon juice, sprinkle with parsley and serve.

Serves: 2-3

Chicken Liver and Rice Balls

1 pound (500 grams) chicken livers
2 cups rice, ground
3 tablespoons chicken stock

½ teaspoon salt
¼ teaspoon black pepper
Pinch of nutmeg

Grind the chicken livers. Combine ½ of the ground liver with the rice and chicken stock. Reserve the remaining liver. Season with salt, pepper and nutmeg. Knead into a dough.

Shape the dough into balls. Press a hole in each with your finger and fill.

Filling

1 onion, chopped
2 scallions (shallots), chopped
Oil for frying

½ teaspoon salt
¼ teaspoon black pepper
½ cup pine nuts

Sauté the onion and scallions in oil until golden. Add to the reserved chicken livers and season with salt and pepper. Brown the pine nuts in oil and combine with the chicken liver mixture. Mix well. Fill the rice balls with the above mixture and seal closed. Sauté in oil until golden.

Serves: 4

Stuffed Quince with Chicken Livers

4 quinces	½ teaspoon salt
2 eggs, beaten	¼ teaspoon black pepper
3 tablespoons bread crumbs	¼ teaspoon oregano
1 tablespoon parsley, finely chopped	Oil for frying

Peel the quinces and cook in boiling water until tender.

Put the cooked quinces through the grinder. Add the eggs, bread crumbs, parsley and seasonings and combine well. Knead the resulting mixture into a dough and shape into squares. Press a hole into each with your finger and fill with liver stuffing. Sauté in oil over a low flame and serve at once.

Filling

2 chicken livers	1 teaspoon tomato purée
2 tablespoons oil	½ teaspoon salt
1 scallion (shallot), chopped	¼ teaspoon black pepper
1 hard-cooked egg yolk	

Sauté the livers in oil. Remove from the pan and reserve. Sauté the chopped scallion in the oil remaining in the pan.

Put the livers, scallion and hard-cooked egg yolk through the grinder. Mix in the tomato purée and season with salt and pepper.

Serves: 4

Sautéed Liver on Toast

4 chicken or 2 turkey livers
2 teaspoons oil
2 apples, sliced crosswise and cored to make 8 apple rings
¼ cup dry red wine

2 tablespoons sugar
8 slices white bread
Oil for frying
¼ teaspoon cinnamon
2 teaspoons chives, chopped

Sauté the liver in oil. Allow to cool and divide into 8 pieces.

Simmer 8 apple rings in the wine and sugar until soft (about 10 minutes). Remove the crust from the bread and fry lightly in oil on both sides. Cut into rounds.

Place the rounds of bread on a serving plate. Cover each with an apple ring dusted with cinnamon and top with a piece of liver. Sprinkle with chopped chives.

Serves: 4

Baked Turkey Balls

6½ pounds (3 kilograms) potatoes, boiled and mashed
4 eggs
3 tablespoons flour
1 teaspoon salt
½ teaspoon black pepper
⅛ teaspoon nutmeg
2 onions, chopped

2 scallions (shallots), chopped
2 tablespoons margarine
1 pound (500 grams) turkey breast, cooked and diced
3 tomatoes, peeled and chopped
1 teaspoon Parmesan cheese
1 teaspoon parsley, chopped
Matzo crumbs

Combine the potatoes, eggs and flour, mixing well. Season with salt, pepper and nutmeg. Reserve.

Sauté the onions and scallions in margarine until golden. Add the turkey, tomatoes, cheese and parsley. Blend thoroughly.

Shape the potato mixture into bite-sized balls and press a small hole into each with your finger. Fill each opening with ½ teaspoon of the turkey mixture, close the holes over and roll in matzo crumbs. Arrange the stuffed balls in a greased baking pan and bake in a medium oven (350°) for ½ hour.

Serves: 4

Turkey, Pecans and Apples Casserole

6 portions turkey meat
1 tablespoon margarine
3 small onions, sliced
2 scallions (shallots), sliced
⅓ cup chicken stock
½ cup currants
¾ cup pecans, shelled
3 carrots, sliced

1 stalk celery, chopped
3 firm apples, peeled and sliced
3 bay leaves
1 teaspoon salt
¼ teaspoon curry powder
1 cup dry white wine
Thin carrot strips

Rinse and dry the turkey. Fry in the margarine until well browned.

Put the turkey portions in a flameproof casserole. Add the onions, scallions and chicken stock. Cover and cook over a low flame for 2 hours. After 1 hour of cooking, add the currants, pecans, carrots, celery, apples and bay leaves. At the same time, combine the salt and curry with the wine and add to the turkey mixture.

Before serving, remove the apples, pecans and currants from the casserole. Mash the apples thoroughly. Mix in the pecans and currants. Garnish the apple purée with carrot strips and serve alongside the turkey.

Serves: 6

Turkey Fingers

¾ pound (375 grams) turkey, boned and skinned
4 cloves garlic
1 scallion (shallot)
2 sprigs parsley
1 slice white bread, soaked in water and squeezed dry
1 teaspoon salt
½ teaspoon black pepper
½ teaspoon lemon juice

5 eggs (1 of them hard-cooked)
1 tablespoon margarine
4 tablespoons matzo meal
½ cup oil
1½ pounds (750 grams) potatoes boiled in their jackets, then skinned
2 zucchini (squash)
2 carrots
Sesame seeds

Put the turkey, garlic, scallion, parsley and bread through the grinder. Season with ½ teaspoon salt, ¼ teaspoon pepper and the lemon juice.

Add 2 eggs and 1 tablespoon matzo meal to the turkey mixture and mix thoroughly. Divide into 12 sausage-shaped portions and fry in hot oil.

Mash the potatoes coarsely with the hard-cooked egg. Reserve.

Boil the zucchini and carrots with the potato-egg mixture. Add 2 eggs, 2 tablespoons matzo meal and the remaining salt and pepper. Combine thoroughly and divide into 12 portions. Coat each of the prepared turkey fingers in this mixture. Arrange in a greased baking pan dusted with the remaining matzo meal and sprinkle with sesame seeds. Bake in a hot oven (400°) in the sauce.

Sauce

6 tomatoes, peeled
1 small onion, chopped
1 hot pepper
1 stalk celery, cut in two

1 carrot, cut in two
1 tablespoon margarine
1 teaspoon flour

Mash and drain the tomatoes. Thin with up to 1½ cups of the reserved cooking liquid. Put in a large saucepan with the onion, hot pepper, celery and carrot and boil for 10 minutes.

Remove the vegetables and discard. Add the margarine and flour. Stir and bring to the boil. Remove from the flame and pour over the turkey fingers.

Serves: 4

Spiced Turkey in Wine Aspic

4 cloves garlic, crushed
1 teaspoon mustard
½ teaspoon black pepper
⅛ teaspoon cayenne pepper
1¼ pounds (625 grams)
turkey breast
Bay leaves

1 scallion (shallot), sliced
1 carrot, sliced
2 stalks celery, sliced and
their leaves
4 sprigs parsley
1 teaspoon salt

Prepare a paste of crushed garlic, mustard, black pepper and cayenne pepper and spread over the turkey breast. Cover with a coating of bay leaves and wrap tightly in a cloth. Refrigerate for 48 hours.

Stew the turkey in water to cover with the scallion, carrot, celery, parsley and salt. When the meat is tender, bone and press to remove all the liquids. Cut into pieces. Prepare the aspic.

Aspic

2 pounds (1 kilogram) beef
shinbone
1½ quarts water
1 teaspoon salt
½ teaspoon black pepper

¼ teaspoon thyme
1 scallion (shallot)
6 cloves garlic, crushed
5 bay leaves
1 cup white wine

Boil the beef in 1½ quarts water with the salt, pepper, thyme and scallion. When the meat is tender and can be easily removed from the bone, add the garlic, bay leaves and white wine. Cook an additional 15 minutes. Remove from the flame. Cut the meat into very small pieces or grind it. Strain the stock and reserve.

To finish

2 eggs, hard-cooked
1 cup canned peas and
carrots, drained

½ pound (250 grams) beef
sausage, cooked and sliced
2 cucumber pickles, sliced
2 tomatoes, sliced

Place a layer of hard-cooked eggs in a deep serving dish. Cover with the prepared beef stock. Chill until firm. Add a layer of peas and carrots, cover with more stock and chill again. Top with a layer of beef and turkey.

Arrange sausage and pickle slices around the sides of the dish, cover the meat with beef stock, top with tomato slices and chill.

When the top layer of aspic is firm, turn out onto a platter and serve.

Serves: 4

Turkey and Wine Casserole

2 pounds (1 kilogram) turkey
breast
3 cups dry red wine
1 bottle Osem sauce (a tangy
steak sauce may be substituted)
2 sticks (250 grams) margarine
1 onion, chopped
3 cloves garlic, chopped
3 whites of leek, chopped
2 tablespoons green pepper,
chopped

4 tablespoons celery, chopped
½ head green cabbage,
shredded
½ pound (250 grams) mushrooms,
sliced
2 bay leaves
1 teaspoon salt
½ teaspoon black pepper
Pinch of nutmeg

Marinate the turkey breast in wine and ½ the sauce overnight. Dry well. Brown the turkey in margarine in a flameproof casserole. Remove to a plate and reserve. Sauté the onion, garlic, leek, green pepper, celery, cabbage and mushrooms in the margarine remaining in the casserole. Add the reserved turkey and the bay leaf to the vegetable mixture. Season with salt, pepper, nutmeg and the remaining sauce. Lower the flame, cover and cook for 2 hours. Serve with rice.

Serves: 4-6

Cold Turkey Salad

¾ pound (375 grams) turkey breast, boned and cooked
2 small heads celery, cooked
2 bunches carrots, cooked
Chicken stock
1 medium potato, peeled
1 cucumber pickle
1 avocado
4 pimientos
1 orange, peeled

2 firm apples, peeled
2 cups mayonnaise
1 teaspoon prepared horseradish
2 tablespoons dry white wine
2 teaspoons sugar
½ teaspoon salt
1 tablespoon capers
¾ cup almonds, slivered
Lettuce leaves

The day before, cook the turkey, celery and carrots in chicken stock. Reserve.

Boil the potato and set aside to cool. Cut the reserved turkey, celery, carrots, pickle, avocado and pimientos into 2-inch strips. Divide the orange into sections and cube the boiled potato and apples.

Combine the mayonnaise, horseradish, wine, sugar and salt. Blend thoroughly. Dress the prepared turkey, fruit and vegetables with the seasoned mayonnaise, add the capers and mix well. Sprinkle with slivered almonds. Refrigerate for 1 hour.

Serve with cabbage leaf garnishes.

Serves: 4

A Celebration of the People

First there are the children

And the children grow up . . .

. . . with their friends

To celebrate there is dancing . . .

. . . and there is making music

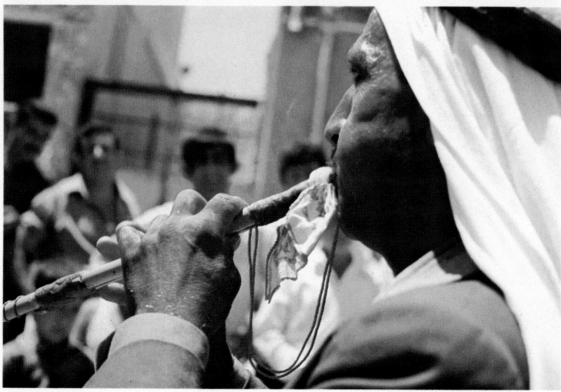

Celebration is rejoicing in the Torah . . .

. . . and lighting the Chanukah candles

The market place at Beersheba...

. . . where some merchants are aggressive . . .

. . . and some are shy

Wedding scene

The bride and her friends are overjoyed . . .

. . . the groom's family is not so sure

Distant relatives from Bukhara arriving for the ceremony

The Wall at last

FISH

Baked Carp Stuffed with Cheese and Mushrooms

A 4½-pound (2 kilogram) carp

Clean fish, cut open lengthwise and salt. Prepare filling and sauce.

Filling

⅓ pound (150 grams) mushrooms	½ cup Gouda cheese, grated
1 medium onion, minced	½ teaspoon salt
3 tablespoons margarine	½ teaspoon black pepper
2 slices white bread, soaked in water and squeezed dry	2 tablespoons oil
	¼ cup water
2 medium tomatoes, chopped	1 tablespoon bread crumbs
	1 tablespoon parsley, chopped

Wash and chop the mushrooms. Sauté with onion in 3 tablespoons margarine. Combine with bread, (cut in pieces), tomato, cheese, salt and pepper. Stuff the fish with the resulting filling and sew up the sides. Place the fish in a baking pan greased with 2 tablespoons oil, add water, sprinkle with bread crumbs and parsley and bake in a medium oven (350°) until the fish turns golden (about ½ hour).

Sauce

1 teaspoon flour	½ cup dry white wine
2 tablespoons water	½ cup Gouda cheese, grated
1½ cups sour cream	

Blend flour and water and stir in the sour cream and wine. Pour over the fish after it turns golden. Top with grated cheese. Return to the oven for 20 minutes.

Serves: 8

Fish Cakes with White Wine

1 package fish fillets
½ avocado, mashed
2 eggs, beaten
1-1½ cups flour
½ cup dry white wine
4 green olives, minced

1 scallion (shallot), grated
1 tablespoon parsley, chopped
½ teaspoon salt
⅛ teaspoon garlic powder
Oil for frying

Grind the fish fillets together with the remaining ingredients. Shape into small cakes. Fry in hot oil.

Serves: 4

Fish and Egg Rolls

6 fish fillets
1½ teaspoons salt
¾ teaspoon black pepper
½ teaspoon thyme
1 tablespoon lime juice
6 eggs, hard-cooked
2 tablespoons flour

2 eggs, beaten
Dash of Worcestershire sauce
Bread crumbs
3 ounces (90 grams) margarine
6 tablespoons cream
1 tablespoon Madeira
1 cup Gouda cheese, grated

Sprinkle the fish fillets on both sides with a mixture of salt, pepper and thyme. Moisten with lime juice.

Place a hard-cooked egg on each fillet. Roll the fish up over the eggs and tie securely with kitchen string. Sprinkle the fish rolls with flour, dip in beaten egg, seasoned with Worcestershire sauce, and coat with bread crumbs. Sauté in 2 ounces (60 grams) margarine, on all sides, until brown.

Transfer the fish to a greased baking dish. Combine the cream and the Madeira. Spoon over the fish rolls. Add the remaining margarine, cut into bits and top with grated cheese. Bake in a medium oven (350°) until the cheese browns (about ½ hour).

Serves: 4

Deep-Fried Fish Balls

1 pound (500 grams) filleted fish	¼ teaspoon black pepper
2 large potatoes, sliced	½ teaspoon mustard powder
1 egg	1 teaspoon lemon juice
1 teaspoon onion, minced	2 tablespoons parsley
½ teaspoon salt	Oil for deep-frying

Cook the fish and potato slices in salted water for 20 minutes. Drain well. Combine the fish and the potatoes. Add the egg, onion, salt, pepper, mustard, lemon juice and parsley.

Shape into balls and deep-fry in hot oil.

Serves: 4

Fish Sandwiches

1 pound (500 grams) fish fillets	1 tablespoon parsley, chopped
Juice of 1 lemon	1½ tablespoons tomato purée
4 scallions (shallots), chopped	⅓ cup Gouda cheese, grated

Divide the fillets into large pieces. Sprinkle with lemon juice and set aside.

Combine the chopped scallions and parsley with the tomato purée. Spread the resulting mixture between two slices of fish, sandwich style. Sprinkle the top of the "sandwich" with grated cheese and place the "sandwich" in a greased baking dish. Repeat with the remaining pieces of fish.

Bake in a medium oven (350°) for 20 minutes, or until fish is well cooked.

Serves: 4

Fish Soufflé

1 pound (500 grams) fish fillets
2 egg yolks
1 cup sour cream
2 tablespoons cracker crumbs
¼ teaspoon salt
¼ teaspoon paprika

⅛ teaspoon nutmeg
Dash of Worcestershire sauce
2 egg whites, beaten until foamy
3 tablespoons Gouda cheese, grated

Cut the fish into small pieces and combine with the egg yolks, sour cream, crumbs, spices and Worcestershire sauce. Gently fold in the egg whites.

Place in a greased soufflé dish or individual dishes. Sprinkle with grated cheese and bake in a moderate oven (325°) for about ½ hour.

Serves: 4

Haddock in Hot Sauce

2 scallions (shallots), chopped
1 tablespoon plus 1 cup oil
3 cloves garlic
1 tablespoon hot red pepper, mashed
2½ cups water
2 small cans tomato paste

⅛ teaspoon cumin
Juice of ½ lemon
½ teaspoon sugar
2 pounds (1 kilogram) fish (haddock)
Green olives

Sauté the scallions in 1 tablespoon oil. Mash the garlic and combine with the red pepper. Dilute this mixture in ¼ cup water. Add to the scallions and stir well. Cook over a medium heat for a few minutes. Add the tomato paste, cumin, lemon juice and sugar. Continue cooking, stirring from time to time, over a low heat for ½ hour. Add the remaining water and oil as needed. When the sauce has thickened, place the fish (whole or in pieces) and the olives in the sauce. Cook an additional 10-15 minutes.

Serves: 4

Fish Salad

1 medium onion, peeled
1 pound (500 grams) fish fillets
1 tablespoon parsley, chopped
Juice of 1 lemon
¼ teaspoon salt
1 large apple, peeled and diced
1 tablespoon walnuts, chopped

2 tablespoons green olives, chopped
1 cup mayonnaise
1 teaspoon mustard
1 teaspoon prepared horseradish
Whole lettuce leaves

Cook the onion in salted water for 10 minutes. Add the fish and continue cooking, over a low flame, until the fish is tender. Reduce the liquid and let the fish cool. Slice the onion.

Cut the fish into small pieces and add to the onion. Mix in the chopped parsley and season with the lemon juice and salt. Add the apple, walnuts and olives. Stir in the mayonnaise, mustard, and horseradish sauce. Chill before serving on lettuce leaves.

Serves: 4

Fish Salad in Vinegar

1 onion, sliced
½ cup water
1 package fish fillets, cut in pieces
½ cup vinegar
1 teaspoon sugar
3 stalks parsley
2 bay leaves
1 teaspoon salt

¼ teaspoon black pepper
3 gherkins, finely diced
1 teaspoon hot red pepper, diced
1 scallion (shallot), finely chopped
Mayonnaise
Mustard
Lettuce leaves
1 lemon, sliced
1 tomato, sliced

Place the onion in a large saucepan with ½ cup water and bring to the boil. Add the pieces of fish and continue cooking for 15 minutes. Add the vinegar, sugar, parsley, bay leaves, salt and pepper. Continue cooking for 1 hour over a low heat.

Drain the cooked fish, transfer to a mixing bowl and mash well with a fork. Add the gherkins, hot red pepper and scallion. Moisten with mayonnaise flavored with a touch of mustard. Shape into the form of a fish and place on a bed of lettuce. Garnish with lemon and tomato slices.

Serves: 2

Spicy Tuna

2 pounds (1 kilogram) fresh tuna
2 tablespoons chives, chopped
2 medium tomatoes, sliced
3 cloves garlic, crushed
½ teaspoon saffron

½ teaspoon salt
2 cups water
1 cup oil of hot red peppers (see page 153) or combine 1 cup oil with cayenne pepper to taste

Clean the fish. Cut into small pieces. Place ½ the chives in a large saucepan. Add the tuna and tomato slices and top with the remaining chives and crushed garlic. Season with saffron and salt. Add the water and seasoned oil. Cook over a medium flame until done (about ½ hour).

Serves: 6

Carp, from the East

1 onion, chopped
1 tablespoon hot pepper, chopped
3 cloves garlic, chopped
2 tablespoons oil
1 tablespoon cumin

½ teaspoon black pepper
1 cup tomato purée
½ cup water
1 pound (500 grams) carp
½ teaspoon salt
2 tablespoons parsley, chopped

Sauté the onion, hot pepper and garlic in the oil. Season with cumin and pepper. Stir in the tomato purée and water. Bring to the boil. Add the pieces of fish and salt. Cook until fish is tender. Sprinkle with parsley.

Serves: 2

Cold Fish in Spicy Lemon Juice

6 medium sized fresh-water fish   2 teaspoons hot red pepper,
1 teaspoon salt   chopped
½ cup oil   6 cloves garlic, chopped
½ cup parsley, chopped   1 bay leaf
1 teaspoon basil   Water
1 cup fresh lemon juice   Lemon slices

Clean the fish thoroughly and salt inside and out. Refrigerate for 2 hours.

Wipe the fish with a dry cloth inside and out. Heat the oil in a deep frying pan and sauté the fish on both sides. Transfer to a second frying pan. Sprinkle with chopped parsley and basil and moisten with lemon juice. Season with chopped hot pepper.

Sauté the chopped garlic in the oil remaining in the first pan, then add the garlic and any remaining oil to the fish mixture. Add a bay leaf and water to cover. Cook over a medium flame until the liquids begin to boil. Lower the flame and continue cooking an additional 15 minutes. Garnish with lemon slices. Serve cold.

Serves: 6

Fish Baked in Wine

2 pounds (1 kilogram) fish fillets   4 medium tomatoes, sliced
1 teaspoon salt   ¼ cup parsley
½ teaspoon black pepper   ½ cup oil
Juice of 1 lemon   1 cup dry white wine
4 cloves garlic, minced   2 tablespoons dry sherry

Season the fish fillets with salt, pepper, lemon juice and garlic. Refrigerate in a closed container for several hours.

Arrange a layer of tomato slices in a deep baking dish. Sprinkle with the parsley. Pour in the oil, wine and sherry. Add the fish fillets. Bake in a hot oven (400°) until the pan liquids are absorbed.

Serves: 6

Baked Fish in *Tehina**

1 tablespoon margarine	*Tehina* (for preparation see
1½ pounds (750 grams) fish	below)
fillets	

Grease a glass baking dish with margarine. Arrange the fish fillets in its bottom. Prepare the *tehina* as follows:

½ pound (250 grams) semi-prepared *tehina*	½ teaspoon salt
	1 tablespoon chopped chives
Juice of 4 lemons	¼ teaspoon mustard powder
2 cloves garlic, crushed	

Cover the fish with the prepared *tehina*. Bake for 1 hour in a medium oven (350°) or until the *tehina* begins to brown at the edges.

Serves: 4

Fish with *Tehina** and Nuts

A 2-pound (1 kilogram) fish	1 tablespoon parsley, chopped
3 tablespoons oil	1 tablespoon pine nuts
2 onions, chopped	*Tehina* (for preparation see
2 scallions (shallots), chopped	below)

Clean the fish carefully and fry in oil. Remove the bones and transfer the fish to a greased baking pan.

Sauté the onions and scallions in the oil remaining in the pan. Scatter over the fish. Sprinkle with parsley and pine nuts. Cover with *tehina,* prepared as follows:

4 tablespoons semi-prepared *tehina*	½-¾ cup water
	5 cloves garlic, finely crushed
Juice of 1 lemon	½ teaspoon salt

Combine the above ingredients into a smooth paste and spread over the fish. Bake in a very hot oven (450°) for 20 minutes.

Serves: 4

* See page 20

Fried Fish in *Tehina**

1 teaspoon salt	2 cloves garlic, chopped
2 pounds (1 kilogram) fish	*Tehina* (for preparation see
½ teaspoon black pepper	below)
1 egg, beaten	1 tablespoon chives, chopped
¼-½ cup oil	Lime slices

Salt the fish and refrigerate for 2 hours. Rinse well and cut into serving pieces. Sprinkle with pepper. Dip each piece in beaten egg and fry in oil. Transfer the fried fish pieces to another pan and sauté the garlic in the oil remaining in the first pan. Reserve.

Prepare the *tehina* as follows:

3 ounces (90 grams) semi-	1 cup water
prepared *tehina*	Juice of ½ lemon

Combine the above ingredients into a smooth paste and add the sautéed garlic and chopped chives.

Top the prepared fish with the prepared *tehina* and cook over a medium flame for 15 minutes. Garnish with lime slices.

* See page 20.   Serves: 4

Fish 'n' Milk Stew

2 cups water, salted
2 scallions (shallots)
¼ cup carrots, sliced
¼ cup peas, raw
¼ teaspoon black pepper
2 pounds (1 kilogram) fish

4 medium potatoes, peeled and sliced
1 cup milk
½ teaspoon margarine
¼ teaspoon paprika

Bring the water to the boil with the scallions, carrots, peas and pepper. Add the fish and potatoes. Cook over a medium heat until all the water has evaporated. Add the milk and margarine. Sprinkle with paprika. Simmer for an additional 10 minutes. Serve hot or cold.

Serves: 4-6

Fish Fillets Baked in Tomato Sauce

4 tablespoons margarine
2 onions, chopped
2 scallions (shallots), chopped
¼ cup green pepper, diced
¼ cup celery, diced
4 cloves garlic, crushed
2 tablespoons flour

3½ cups tomatoes, chopped
¼ cup parsley, chopped
⅓ cup tomato purée
1 bay leaf
Salt and black pepper to taste
6 fish fillets

Melt the margarine in a large saucepan and add the onions, scallions, green pepper, celery and garlic. Cook gently for 5 minutes. Stir in the flour, tomatoes, parsley, tomato purée and bay leaf. Season with salt and pepper. Simmer over a low flame for 20 minutes.

Salt the fish fillets and arrange them in a greased baking dish. Cover with the prepared sauce and bake in a medium oven (350°) for about ½ hour.

Serves: 6

Curried Fish and Rice

1½ pounds (750 grams) fish
½ teaspoon salt
3 tablespoons oil
1¾ cups water
3 ounces (90 grams) margarine
1 tablespoon tomato paste

½ teaspoon lemon peel, grated
1 cup rice
9 scallions (shallots), sliced
4 tomatoes, sliced
½ teaspoon curry powder

Clean the fish. Split lengthwise and cut into pieces. Sprinkle with ½ teaspoon salt. Fry in 2 tablespoons hot oil until golden.

Combine 1½ cups water, the margarine, tomato paste, lemon peel and remaining salt in a saucepan. Bring to the boil. Add the rice and cook over a high flame 5-10 minutes (until the rice absorbs most of the water). Lower the flame and continue cooking until the rice swells.

Grease a large, flameproof casserole with the remaining oil. Line with the sliced scallions, cover with a layer of tomatoes and sprinkle with curry powder. Top with ¾ of the fish.

Bone the remaining fish and break into small pieces. Add these to the rice. Spread the resulting mixture over the layer of fish. Cover the casserole and cook over a high flame for 15 minutes or until the scallions have browned. Lower the flame, add the remaining water and cook for an additional 1½ hours. Add more water, a tablespoon at a time, if needed.

Serve turned out on a platter, with the rice on the bottom and the scallions on top.

Serves: 4

109

Fish Stuffed with Walnuts

4 small fish 1 scallion (shallot), chopped
1 cup walnuts, crushed 2 teaspoons lime juice
¼ teaspoon salt Oil for frying
2 tablespoons parsley, chopped Lettuce leaves

Prepare the fish for stuffing.

Combine the nuts, salt, parsley, scallion and lime juice. Blend well. Sauté the resulting mixture in oil for 5 minutes while stirring. Set aside to cool.

Stuff the fish with the prepared filling. Fry the stuffed fish in oil on both sides. Serve on lettuce leaves.

Serves: 4

Minted Fish

2 scallions (shallots), chopped 2 teaspoons green pepper, finely
2 cloves garlic, finely chopped diced
2 tablespoons oil 1½ pounds (750 grams) fish
2 cups water ¼ teaspoon black pepper
1 small can tomato paste 6 mint leaves
¼ teaspoon salt 1 tablespoon parsley, chopped
2 teaspoons carrot, finely diced

Sauté the scallions and garlic in oil until golden. Combine the water, tomato paste and salt and add to the scallion mixture. Stir in the carrot and peppers and cook for 10 minutes. Divide the fish into pieces and add to the sauce. Season with pepper and add the mint leaves and parsley. Cook over a low flame for 1 hour.

Serves: 4

Stuffed Fish with Vegetables

A 2-pound (1 kilogram) fish
½ lemon
2 cloves garlic
½ teaspoon salt
¼ teaspoon black pepper
1 teaspoon Worcestershire sauce
1 pound (500 grams) potatoes, cooked and mashed

Onion slices
Tomato slices
1 tablespoon parsley, chopped
1 teaspoon oil
1 pound (500 grams) green beans
½ pound (250 grams) carrots
1 pound (500 grams) turnips

Cut the fish and rinse well. Rub the outside of the fish with ½ lemon. Crush the garlic, combine it with the salt and pepper and spread it over the outside of the fish. Fill the inside of the fish with a mixture of boned fish, Worcestershire sauce and mashed potatoes. Place the stuffed fish in a greased baking pan and decorate the top with onion and tomato slices. Sprinkle with chopped parsley and top with 1 teaspoon oil.

Parboil the vegetables in salted water. Drain them and set aside. When they have cooled, cut them into pieces and place them around the fish. Bake in a hot oven (400°) for ½ hour, or until the fish is done.

Serves: 6

Roasted Sardines

1 pound (500 grams) fresh sardines
2 scallions (shallots), sliced
½ teaspoon salt

¼ teaspoon black pepper
Juice of 1 lemon
2 tablespoons parsley, chopped
½ cup oil

Clean the fish well, removing the heads. Place half the scallions in a buttered baking dish. Cover with half the sardines. Sprinkle with salt and pepper. Cover with the remaining scallions and top with the rest of the sardines. Sprinkle with lemon juice and parsley. Cover with oil.

Roast in a low oven (275°) for 1 hour, or until the fish browns.

Serves: 4

Savoury Jellied Fish

A 3-pound (1½ kilogram) fish   1 small onion, sliced
2 cups water   ½ teaspoon basil
1 cup dry white wine   1 inch lemon rind
3 tablespoons oil   Celery leaves
1 teaspoon salt   1 tablespoon lemon juice
¼ teaspoon black pepper   4 packages gelatine
4 bay leaves   Watercress

Garnishes:

Deviled eggs   Black and green olives
Parsley sprigs   Chopped jellied aspic

Slit the fish lengthwise and wrap it carefully in a cloth to prevent it from crumbling as it cooks.

Combine the water, wine, oil, salt, pepper, bay leaves, onion, basil, lemon rind and celery leaves in a large pan. Poach the fish in this mixture for 15 minutes.

Remove the fish from the poaching liquid. Bone it and arrange it in a deep serving dish. Strain the poaching liquid and add 1 tablespoon lemon juice. Allow to cool then bring to the boil and add the gelatine. When the gelatine has melted, remove from the flame and chill until the mixture is semi-firm. Pour over the fish. Decorate the serving dish with watercress and surround the fish with the garnishes.

Serves: 4

Cold Stuffed Fish

A 2-pound (1 kilogram) fish
2 onions, chopped
3 tablespoons oil
1 potato, boiled
½ teaspoon salt
¼ teaspoon black pepper
1 teaspoon sugar

1 teaspoon prepared horseradish
3 egg whites
2 tablespoons water
4 scallions (shallots)
1 carrot
1 stalk celery

Gut and bone the fish, being careful to leave the skin intact. Sauté the onions in 2 tablespoons oil and put them through the grinder with the fish flesh and potato. Season with salt, pepper, sugar and horseradish.

Beat the egg whites until foamy. Fold into the fish mixture along with 2 tablespoons water and the remaining oil. Stuff the fish skin with the resulting mixture.

Place the scallions, carrot and celery in a large pan. Add the fish and cover with water. Cook for 2 hours, adding water as needed. Remove from heat. Let the fish cool before serving.

Serves: 4

Baked Fish with Cheese

1-pound (500 grams) fish
½ teaspoon salt
1 teaspoon lime juice
4 large tomatoes, sliced
½ teaspoon black pepper
4 tablespoons potatoes, diced
2 gherkins, diced

2 scallions (shallots), chopped
1 tablespoon celery, chopped
2 teaspoons margarine
4 slices American cheese
1 cup dry white wine
1 tablespoon almonds, chopped

Clean and bone the fish. Salt inside and out. Sprinkle with lime juice.

Place the layer of tomato slices in a greased baking dish. Cover with a layer of fish. Sprinkle with pepper and with a mixture of potatoes, gherkins, scallions and celery. Dot with bits of margarine. Bake in a medium oven (350°) about 40 minutes.

5 minutes before the fish is done, top with a layer of cheese slices. Remove from oven, pour on the wine, sprinkle with chopped almonds and serve at once.

Serves: 2

Fish Stuffed with Eggplant

3 fresh-water fish	½ cup oil
2 teaspoons salt	2 scallions (shallots), chopped
¾ teaspoon black pepper	2 bay leaves
¼ cup lime juice	

Prepare the fish for stuffing. Sprinkle inside and out with 1½ teaspoons salt and ½ teaspoon black pepper.

Combine the lime juice, oil, scallions, bay leaves and the remaining salt and pepper. Soak the fish in this marinade overnight, turning occasionally. Prepare the filling.

Filling

2 medium eggplants	1 teaspoon salt
3 eggs, hard-cooked and mashed	½ teaspoon black pepper
2 ounces (60 grams) Feta cheese	½ teaspoon cumin
2 tablespoons bread crumbs	1 tablespoon mayonnaise
1 tablespoon chives, chopped	1 teaspoon lemon juice
2 cloves garlic, crushed	1 teaspoon olive oil
¼ teaspoon mustard	

Parboil the eggplants. Scrape off the peel and mash the pulp. Combine with the remaining ingredients, blending thoroughly.

To assemble

2 scallions (shallots), chopped	5 green olives, chopped
1 tablespoon oil for frying	2 tomatoes, sliced
1 clove garlic, crushed	3 pimientos, cut into strips

Remove the fish from the marinade and fill with the eggplant mixture. Reserve the marinade. Sauté the scallions in oil until golden in a large frying pan. Add the remaining ingredients and cook over a low flame for 5 minutes. Place the resulting mixture in the bottom of a greased baking pan.

Arrange the stuffed fish on the tomato mixture. Cover with the reserved marinade and bake in a 350° oven for 45 minutes.

To finish

10 ounces (300 grams) Feta cheese
1 pint cream
2 eggs, hard-cooked and mashed
1 tablespoon mayonnaise
1 tablespoon oil
½ teaspoon mustard
½ teaspoon paprika
½ teaspoon salt

¼ teaspoon black pepper
2 tablespoons onion, chopped
2 tablespoons parsley, chopped
1 cucumber pickle, diced
American cheese slices
2 ounces (60 grams) pine nuts
Black and green olives, sliced
Pimiento strips

Mash the cheese and combine with the cream and eggs. Blend thoroughly. Mix in the mayonnaise, oil, mustard, paprika, salt, pepper, onion, parsley and pickle. Combine to form a sauce.

After ¾ hour remove the fish from the oven. Cover with cheese slices, pour on the sauce and sprinkle with the pine nuts. Garnish with sliced olives and pimiento strips.

Return to the oven and bake an additional 15 minutes. Serve at once.

Serves: 6

Sautéed Carp Eggs

1 pound (500 grams) fresh water fish eggs
3 tablespoons matzo meal
2 teaspoons chives, finely chopped
1 egg, beaten

3 tablespoons oil
3 cloves garlic, crushed
1 cup tomato juice
1 cup sweet white wine
1 tablespoon lemon juice

Divide the carp eggs into 8 portions. Coat each portion with matzo meal mixed with the chives, dip in the beaten egg and sauté in oil on both sides. Add the remaining ingredients and simmer over a low flame for 5 minutes. Serve on a bed of lettuce.

Serves: 4

Fish Baked in Pomegranate Juice and Wine

3 pounds (1½ kilograms) fish
2 teaspoons salt
3 ounces (90 grams) almonds, blanched and slivered
1 small can mushrooms, drained and chopped
¼ cup bread crumbs
2 cloves garlic, crushed
1 tablespoon parsley, chopped

¼ teaspoon black pepper
½ cup Rhine wine, or other light white wine
½ cup pomegranate juice (semi-sweetened lime juice may be substituted)
¼ cup dry white vermouth
2 onions, sliced
1 ounce (30 grams) margarine

Clean the fish and slit them open along the sides. Salt well. Set aside for 10 minutes then rinse.

Arrange the fish in a well-greased baking pan. Combine the almonds, mushrooms, bread crumbs, garlic, parsley and pepper in a mixing bowl. Mix thoroughly and spread over the fish. Moisten with the wine, pomegranate or lime juice and vermouth. Top with onion slices. Dot with margarine.

Bake in a hot oven (400°) for 45 minutes, basting from time to time with the pan juices.

Serves: 6

Codfish Paprikash, Hungarian Style

2 pounds (1 kilogram) codfish
½ stick (60 grams) margarine
2 scallions (shallots), chopped
1 clove garlic, chopped
1 green pepper, seeded and diced

1 large tomato, chopped
¼ cup fennel, chopped
Salt and black pepper to taste
1 tablespoon paprika
Chopped parsley

Simmer the cod in boiling water for 1 hour. Drain. Cut into 2-inch cubes.

Melt the margarine in a large frying pan. Add the scallions, garlic, pepper, tomato and fennel. Season with salt and pepper. Stir in the paprika and blend thoroughly.

Simmer over a low flame for 15 minutes. Add the fish and simmer an additional 15 minutes. Sprinkle with parsley and serve at once.

Serves: 6

Carp, Chinese Style

1 pound (500 grams) carp	¼ cup flour
½ teaspoon salt	½ cup oil
¼ teaspoon black pepper	

Split the carp in half, lengthwise. Bone. Divide into 10 pieces. Season with salt and pepper. Roll in flour. Sauté in oil. Arrange in a deep serving platter. Prepare the sauce.

Sauce

4 scallions (shallots), thinly sliced	½ small can tomato paste
1 pound (500 grams) carrots, thinly sliced	¼ cup sugar
	1½ cups water
	Juice of 1 lemon
9 bay leaves	¼ cup parsley, chopped

Place the scallions, carrots, bay leaves, tomato paste, sugar, water and lemon juice in a large saucepan. Cook over a high flame for ½ hour.

Pour the prepared sauce over the fish. Sprinkle with chopped parsley. Refrigerate 1 hour before serving.

Serves: 4

Codfish with Chick Peas

2 cups chick peas
¼ teaspoon baking soda
3 cups chicken stock
2 pimientos, chopped
1 small onion, minced
1 green pepper, seeded and
    chopped
2 chili peppers, seeded and
    chopped

3 pounds (1½ kilograms) codfish
1 teaspoon salt
½ teaspoon black pepper
1 teaspoon paprika
5 tablespoons oil
1 cup tomato juice
2 cloves garlic, minced
2 tablespoons parsley, chopped

Soak the chick peas and soda overnight in water to cover. Drain.

Peel the chick peas and transfer to a pressure cooker. Cook in 3 cups chicken stock, over a medium flame, for 15 minutes.

Place the chick peas, chopped pimientos, onion, chopped green pepper and chili peppers in a flameproof casserole. Add the fish. Season with salt, pepper and paprika. Moisten with oil and tomato juice. Sprinkle with garlic and parsley. Cook over a medium flame for ½ hour. Serve at once.

Serves: 4

Fried Fish, Spanish Style

A 2-pound (1-kilogram) carp
3 tablespoons oil
1 carrot, thinly sliced
1 stalk fennel, chopped
½ cup almonds, slivered

Juice of 3 lemons
2 teaspoons sugar
½ teaspoon salt
1½ cups water

Remove the heads from the fish. Cut the fish into pieces and sauté the cut-up fish in hot oil.

Place a layer of sliced carrot and chopped fennel in a greased baking dish. Add the fish. Sprinkle with parsley and almonds. Moisten with lemon juice. Add the sugar, salt and water.

Bake in a medium oven (350°) for ½ hour, or until the pan liquids are absorbed.

Serve hot or cold.

Serves: 6

Tuna in Orange Sauce

3 pounds (1½ kilograms) tuna
2 teaspoons salt
2 teaspoons paprika
1 tomato, peeled and mashed
2 scallions (shallots), chopped
½ stick (60 grams) margarine,
melted
¼ teaspoon celery salt

⅛ teaspoon oregano
Juice of 2 oranges
1 tablespoon lime juice
2 oranges, sliced
1 tablespoon green pepper,
chopped
1 tablespoon sweet red pepper,
chopped

Clean and bone the fish. Sprinkle with salt and paprika. Refrigerate for 3 hours.

Combine the tomato and scallions. Add the margarine, celery salt, oregano and fruit juices. Blend thoroughly.

Line a glass baking dish with orange slices. Add the tuna, cover with the fruit juice mixture and sprinkle with chopped peppers. Bake in a medium oven (350°) for 1 hour.

Serves: 6

Codfish and Mushrooms

¼ pound (125 grams) mushrooms
½ stick (60 grams) margarine
½ clove garlic, chopped
3 pounds (1½ kilograms) codfish, cut into pieces
1 teaspoon salt

½ teaspoon black pepper
1 can cream of mushroom soup, condensed
1 cup milk
½ pint sour cream
Paprika

Wash and peel the mushrooms. Sauté in ¼ of the margarine with the garlic. Reserve.

Melt the remaining margarine in a flameproof casserole. Add the fish. Season with salt and pepper.

Dilute the mushroom soup with milk. Pour over the fish. Add the sour cream, cover and cook over a low flame for 15 minutes.

Add the mushrooms and garlic. Transfer the casserole to a medium oven (350°). Bake for 5 minutes. Sprinkle with paprika and serve at once.

Serves: 6

Fish and Apricots

8 scallions (shallots), cut into thin rings
2 tablespoons oil
½ teaspoon salt
¼ teaspoon black pepper
2 teaspoons paprika

6 fish fillets
12 dried apricots, halved
6 tomatoes, halved horizontally
2 tablespoons tomato juice
1 teaspoon sugar
Juice of ½ lemon

Sauté the scallion rings in oil in a large frying pan until golden. Season with salt, pepper and paprika.

Arrange the fish fillets in the pan, cut-side down. Cover the fish with apricot and tomato halves. Add the tomato juice. Cover and cook over a medium flame for 15 minutes.

Sprinkle the fish with 1 teaspoon sugar. When it melts, moisten with lemon juice. Slip the pan under the broiler and broil until the top browns.

Serve hot or cold.

Serves: 6

Codfish, Israeli Style

12 slices codfish	¼ teaspoon black pepper
1 cup flour	½ cup beer
2 egg yolks	½ teaspoon mustard
½ teaspoon salt	Oil for frying

Rinse the fish and pat dry with a cloth. Reserve.

Dilute the flour in a little water. Blend into a thick paste. Add the egg yolks, one by one. Season with salt and pepper. Slowly incorporate the beer and mustard, combining well.

Dip the reserved fish slices in the egg mixture and sauté in oil. Place the sautéed fish on paper towels to drain. Serve hot with avocado sauce.

Avocado Sauce

1 tablespoon oil	2 avocados, peeled
1 tablespoon margarine	Salt and black pepper
3 tablespoons scallions	to taste
(shallots), chopped	½ cup chicken stock
1 clove garlic, crushed	1 teaspoon lemon juice

Heat the oil and margarine in a small frying pan. Add the scallions and garlic and sauté. Reserve.

Force the avocado through a strainer. Mash the sautéed scallions and garlic and pass through a strainer along with the oil remaining in the pan. Add to the avocados. Stir well. Season with salt and pepper, moisten with chicken stock and lemon juice and heat over a low flame, stirring constantly. Pour over the fish. Serve at once.

Serves: 6

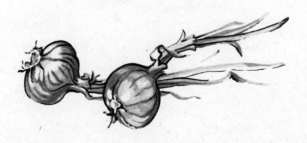

Codfish Roll

1 pound (500 grams) codfish	1 teaspoon salt
2 scallions (shallots), chopped	½ teaspoon curry powder
4 eggs, separated	⅛ teaspoon cayenne pepper
1 tablespoon parsley, chopped	Dash of Worcestershire sauce
2 tablespoons lime juice	Bread crumbs
2 tablespoons lemon juice	1 cup Parmesan cheese, grated
1 tablespoon oil	Grapefruit and orange sections

Grind the fish. Place in a mixing bowl and add the scallions, egg yolks, parsley, lime juice, lemon juice and oil. Blend thoroughly. Season with salt, curry powder, cayenne pepper and Worcestershire sauce. Fold in the egg whites, whipped stiff.

Shape the fish mixture into a large patty and coat with bread crumbs. Place in a greased baking dish. Bake in a hot oven (400°) for ½ hour. Sprinkle the patty with grated cheese and roll it up tightly. Place on a serving dish. Slice, garnish with grapefruit and orange sections and serve at once.

Accompany with green peas or a red cabbage salad.

Serves: 4

Fish in Orange Sauce

1 orange
2 tablespoons margarine
¼ cup fennel, chopped
1 tablespoon scallion, chopped

½ cup toast crumbs, seasoned
with ½ teaspoon celery salt
1 teaspoon salt
¼ teaspoon black pepper
6 fish fillets

Peel half of the orange. Cut the peel into thin strips and reserve. Remove the remaining peel and discard. Seed the orange, separate it into sections and chop the fruit into small pieces.

Melt the margarine in a saucepan. Add the fennel and scallion. Cook until tender. Stir in the chopped orange and seasoned toast crumbs. Blend thoroughly.

Salt and pepper the fish fillets. Dip them one by one into the cooked orange mixture, then roll them up and secure with kitchen string. Prepare the sauce.

Sauce

2 cups orange juice
1 teaspoon sugar
¼ teaspoon salt
¼ teaspoon ginger

½ teaspoon prepared horseradish
1 tablespoon cornstarch
Orange slices

Heat the orange juice, reserved orange peel, sugar, salt, ginger and horse-radish in a large saucepan. When the mixture comes to the boil, add the prepared fish rolls. Poach for 15-20 minutes.

Remove the fish to a serving platter.

Dilute the cornstarch in a little water. Add to the orange juice mixture and stir over a low flame until the sauce thickens. Pour the sauce over the fish, garnish with orange slices and serve at once.

Serves: 6

Baked Fish and Eggplant

1 pound (500 grams) eggplant	2 tablespoons parsley, chopped
2 teaspoons salt	4 eggs
2 scallions (shallots), chopped	½ teaspoon cumin
1 clove garlic, chopped	½ teaspoon black pepper
Oil for frying	1 teaspoon lime juice
1 pound (500 grams) fish fillets	Flour
1 slice white bread, soaked in water and squeezed dry	

Slice the eggplant. Sprinkle with salt and set aside for 15 minutes.

Sauté the scallions and garlic in oil. Add the fish and sauté lightly. Remove from flame. Flake the fish and combine the fish, scallions and garlic with the bread, parsley and 1 beaten egg. Blend thoroughly. Season with cumin, pepper and lime juice.

Dip the reserved eggplant slices in flour. Sauté in oil.

Place ½ the sautéed eggplant in the bottom of a greased baking dish. Add the fish mixture. Cover with the rest of the eggplant. Beat the remaining eggs and pour over the prepared mixture.

Bake in a medium oven (350°) for ½ hour.

Serves: 4

MEAT
(Lamb, Beef, Veal)

Pumpkin Stuffed with Lamb and Currants

2 small pumpkins
1 cup lean lamb, ground
½ cup onion, chopped
¼ cup oil
1 cup rice, boiled
¾ cup pine nuts
¾ cup currants
½ teaspoon salt
¼ teaspoon black pepper
½ teaspoon curry powder

Wash the pumpkins well. Hollow them out carefully, reserving their caps to use as covers.

Sauté the ground meat and onion in oil. Add the remaining ingredients and continue to cook, stirring constantly. When the mixture is well blended, transfer it to the prepared pumpkin cases. Cover with the reserved caps. Bake in a medium oven (350°) for 20-30 minutes.

Serves: 8

Beef "Dates"

⅔ pound (300 grams) lean beef, ground
4 cloves garlic, crushed
1 teaspoon hot green pepper, minced
1 tablespoon celery, finely chopped
1 tablespoon parsley, chopped
1 teaspoon cumin
Salt and black pepper to taste
1 tablespoon oil plus ½ cup
3 eggs, hard-cooked and sliced
1 teaspoon tomato paste
⅛ teaspoon oregano

Combine the ground meat with the garlic, hot green pepper, celery, parsley, cumin, salt and pepper. Blend in 1 tablespoon oil and mix thoroughly. Shape the meat mixture into the form of large dates. Make an opening in each "date" and insert a slice of hard-cooked egg. Press closed.

Put ½ cup oil in a flameproof casserole and blend in the tomato paste. Add the oregano. Arrange the beef "dates" in the casserole side by side. Cover and cook over a low flame until the meat juices evaporate.

Serves: 2

Beef Pancake

2 potatoes, boiled and peeled
1 teaspoon onion, grated
6 eggs, beaten
½ teaspoon salt
¼ teaspoon black pepper

1 cup lean beef, minced
1 tablespoon parsley, finely chopped
Oil for frying
½ teaspoon paprika

Combine the potatoes, onion, eggs, salt, pepper, lamb, and parsley. Mix well. Heat the oil in a deep frying pan. When it begins to smoke, add the meat mixture. Sauté on both sides over a low flame. Turn out onto a platter, sprinkle with paprika and cut into 4 portions.

Serves: 4

Sausages in Blankets

10 ounces (300 grams) lean beef
3 slices white bread, soaked in water and squeezed dry
2 scallions (shallots)
1 egg, hard-cooked
5 cloves garlic

¼ cup parsley
1 teaspoon salt
½ teaspoon black pepper
Small beef sausages (allow 2-3 per person)
Oil for frying

Put the meat, bread, scallions, egg and garlic through the grinder. Add the parsley, salt and pepper and combine well.

Cook the sausages in boiling water for 5 minutes. Dry them thoroughly and wrap them in individual "blankets" of the ground meat mixture. Place the wrapped sausages in a greased frying pan and brown gently on all sides.

Lamb Rolls

2 cups flour
1 tablespoon oil
1 tablespoon vinegar
½ teaspoon salt
¾ cup water

3 ounces (90 grams) margarine, softened
1 egg, beaten or 2 tablespoons oil

Knead the flour, oil, vinegar, salt and water into a smooth, soft dough. Roll it out and coat the surface with margarine. Fold the greased dough over and grease it again. Keep folding and greasing until the dough is the size of a large pancake. Refrigerate for ½ hour.

Roll out the dough again and cut it into a series of circles, using the rim of a glass. Fill each circle with filling and seal it closed. Place the meat rolls in a pan. Spread a beaten egg or oil over the top and bake in a medium oven (350°) until brown (about ½ hour).

Filling

1¼ cup lean lamb, ground
1 onion, chopped and sautéed in 2 tablespoons oil
1 teaspoon gherkins, finely chopped

½ teaspoon mustard
½ teaspoon salt
¼ teaspoon black pepper

Combine the above ingredients and mix thoroughly.

Serves: 4

Stuffed Grape Leaves

1 pound (500 grams) grape
leaves
¾ cup lamb, minced
¾ cup rice
3 cloves garlic, crushed
1 tablespoon dill, finely
chopped

1 tablespoon parsley, finely
chopped
1 tablespoon tomato purée
¼ cup pine nuts
Salt and black pepper to taste
Chicken stock
1 tablespoon sugar
2 tablespoons lemon juice

Soften the grape leaves in boiling water (about 2 minutes). Combine the meat, rice, garlic, dill, parsley, tomato purée and pine nuts. Mix well. Season with salt and pepper to taste.

Spread open the leaves and place 2 teaspoons of the prepared filling, rolled into a ball, near the broad end of each. Fold over the left and right sides of the leaf until they meet, then roll up the leaf, starting just beyond the filled area and working toward the tip.

Place the stuffed leaves side by side in a flameproof casserole, seam-side down. Cover with chicken stock, the sugar and lemon juice and cook for 15 minutes over a high flame. Lower the flame and continue cooking for 1 hour.

Serves: 4

Beef and Mayonnaise Fondue

Mayonnaise
Mustard
Capers
Crushed garlic
Curry powder
Tomato juice

Chopped onion
Chopped pickle
Oil for deep-frying
3 pounds (1½ kilograms) filet of
beef, cut into ¾-inch cubes
Lettuce and tomato salad

Prepare a variety of mayonnaise sauces: mayonnaise with mustard and capers, mayonnaise with crushed garlic, mayonnaise with curry, mayonnaise with tomato juice and chopped onion, mayonnaise with chopped pickle.

Heat the oil in a deep metal pot in the middle of the dining table. Each guest cooks his pieces of meat by dipping them into the boiling oil with the aid of a long fork. The meat is then dipped into the sauces of one's choice.

Accompany with a seasoned tomato and lettuce salad.

Serves: 6

Veal and Vegetable Rolls

1 pound (500 grams) veal cutlet	1 cucumber pickle, diced
4 tomatoes, chopped	2 stalks celery, chopped
1 green pepper, seeded and diced	1 tablespoon parsley, chopped
	½ teaspoon salt
2 small onions, finely chopped	⅛ teaspoon black pepper

Pound the cutlets until thin. Combine the prepared vegetables and add the parsley, salt and pepper. Mix well. Prepare the sauce (see below). Fill the cutlets with the vegetable mixture and fold them closed. Tie up each stuffed cutlet with string. Place the veal rolls side by side in a deep saucepan. Simmer in the prepared sauce for ½ hour.

Sauce

1 onion, grated	1 teaspoon lemon juice
2 teaspoons oil	1 bay leaf
1 carrot, grated	2 cups tomato juice

Sauté the onion in oil. Add the grated carrot and continue to cook for 3 minutes. Stir in the lemon juice, bay leaf and tomato juice. Blend thoroughly and pour over the veal rolls.

Serves: 2

Ground Meat in *Tehina**

1 pound (500 grams) lean meat, ground
1 teaspoon salt
½ teaspoon black pepper
1 teaspoon Worcestershire sauce
1 tablespoon chives, chopped
Tehina (for preparation see below)

Cook the ground meat over a low flame with the salt and pepper for 10 minutes. Stir occasionally to prevent sticking. Remove from heat and allow to cool. Mix in the Worcestershire sauce and chives and place in a baking dish. Prepare the *tehina*.

To prepare *tehina*:

3 ounces (90 grams) semi-prepared *tehina*
Pinch of cayenne pepper
Juice of 1 lemon
4 cloves garlic, crushed
1 tablespoon parsley, chopped
¼ cup water
⅓ teaspoon salt

Mix the above ingredients together thoroughly. Refrigerate for 2 hours to thicken. Spread the prepared *tehina* over the meat mixture and bake in a medium oven (350°) until the *tehina* begins to brown (about 1 hour). Drain away any accumulating meat liquids.

Serves: 2

*See page 20.

Beef Goulash with Prunes

1½ pounds (750 grams) beef (round steak or shinbone) cut into 1-inch cubes
3 scallions (shallots), chopped
½ cup oil
1 teaspoon salt
½ teaspoon paprika
1 cup beef stock
¼ cup currants
½ pound (250 grams) dried prunes or ½ pound (250 grams) canned prunes, drained

Brown the meat and scallions in oil in a flameproof casserole. Stir in the salt, paprika and ¼ cup stock. Cover and simmer for 1½ hours, adding additional stock as needed to prevent the meat from scorching.

Meanwhile soak the currants and the prunes (if they are dried) in water for ½ hour. Add the prunes and the currants to the casserole 20 minutes before the meat is done.

Serves: 6

Stuffed Beet Leaves

2 pounds (1 kilogram) large beet leaves
2 cups lean beef, ground
1 tablespoon parsley, finely chopped
1 teaspoon cumin
1 teaspoon prepared horse-radish
½ teaspoon mustard
2½ cups water
1 teaspoon salt
¼ teaspoon black pepper
2 tablespoons matzo meal
1 egg, beaten
Oil for frying
Juice of 1 lemon

Wash the leaves well and soak in water for 15 minutes. Drain.

Combine the meat, parsley, cumin, horseradish and mustard with ½ cup water. Blend thoroughly, seasoning with ½ teaspoon salt and ¼ teaspoon pepper.

Place 2 teaspoons of the prepared filling on each beef leaf and roll up the leaves (see page 130). Secure the leaf packages with toothpicks. Dip each stuffed leaf first in matzo meal, then in beaten egg. Sauté gently until brown. Remove the toothpicks.

Place the sautéed leaf packages side by side in flameproof casserole, seam-side down. Add the remaining water, the rest of the salt and the lemon juice. Cook until the water is reduced to covering the bottom of the dish.

Serves: 4

Veal Pot Roast with Apricots

1 pound (500 grams) apricots,
dried or canned
1 large onion, chopped
3 scallions (shallots), chopped
¼ cup oil
¼ cup raisins
1 clove
1 tablespoon sugar

1 teaspoon salt
½ teaspoon cinnamon
1 pound (500 grams) potatoes,
peeled and sliced
1½ cups chicken stock
A 1-pound (500-gram) piece of
boneless veal, sliced into
6 portions

Soak the apricots (if they are dried) in water overnight. Add the raisins for the last ½ hour.

Sauté the onion and scallions in oil in a flameproof casserole until golden. Add the apricots and ½ cup of their soaking liquid (if they are dried). If you are using canned apricots, substitute ½ cup apricot syrup from the can. Stir in the raisins, clove, sugar, salt, cinnamon, potatoes, chicken stock and veal. Cover and cook over a high flame for 15 minutes. Lower the flame and continue cooking until the liquids evaporate and the meat is tender (about 1 hour).

Serves: 6

Lamb with Olives

2 pounds (1 kilogram) green
olives, pitted
1 pound (500 grams) lean
stewing lamb, sliced
1 onion, chopped
¼ cup oil
1 cup chicken stock

3 cloves garlic, crushed
2 tablespoons celery,
diced
2 tablespoons tomato paste
Pinch of cayenne pepper
1 teaspoon salt
Juice of 1 lemon

Cook the olives in boiling water for 3 minutes to remove their bitterness. Drain well.

Brown the lamb and onion in oil in a flameproof casserole. Add the stock, garlic, celery, tomato paste and cayenne pepper. Cover and simmer for 1 hour over a low flame. Add the salt and lemon juice. Continue cooking for 1 more hour. Add additional stock if needed.

Serves: 4

Ground Beef and Apple Casserole

¾ pound (375 grams) lean beef, ground
2 tablespoons fennel, finely chopped
2 scallions (shallots), minced
6 apples, peeled and cubed
2 tomatoes, peeled and chopped
4 pimientoes, chopped
2 ounces (60 grams) pecans, ground
Salt and black pepper to taste

Combine the above ingredients and blend thoroughly. Place in a greased baking dish. Bake in a medium oven (350°) for 2 hours.

Accompany with a salad of sliced avocados, small black olives and hearts of palm.

Serves: 2

Braised Beef with Vegetables

1 pound (500 grams) beef shoulder, rump or brisket, cut into 1-inch cubes
2 scallions (shallots), chopped
1 stick (125 grams) margarine
½ pound (250 grams) fresh spinach, washed, drained and finely chopped
½ pound (250 grams) white of leek, finely chopped
6 sprigs parsley
A handful of Chinese parsley leaves
10 celery leaves
Juice of 1 lime
1 teaspoon salt
½ teaspoon black pepper
½ teaspoon saffron
½ teaspoon cumin
1 cup beef stock

Sauté the meat pieces and scallions in margarine in a flameproof casserole.

Add the spinach, leek, parsley and celery leaves. Cook slowly until the vegetables have rendered all their water.

Add the lime juice, salt, pepper, saffron and cumin. Pour in the beef stock. Cover and cook over a low flame until the meat softens (about 1½ hours).

Serves: 3

Piquant Braised Lamb with Wine Sauce

1½ pounds (750 grams) leg of lamb, cut into 1-inch cubes
2 tablespoons oil or 3 tablespoons margarine
3 cloves garlic, chopped
2 scallions (shallots), chopped
3 tomatoes, chopped or 2 tablespoons tomato paste
3 hot peppers, chopped
1 cucumber, sliced
¼ cup celery, chopped

1 cup chicken stock
1 teaspoon caraway seeds
½ teaspoon salt
¼ teaspoon black pepper
Pinch of cayenne pepper
1 tablespoon tomato ketchup
¼ cup dry white wine
2 teaspoons flour
1 teaspoon mustard
½ cup green olives, chopped
1 cucumber pickle, chopped

Brown the meat in oil or margarine in a flameproof casserole with the garlic and scallions. Add the tomatoes, or tomato paste, hot peppers, cucumber and celery. Lower the flame and cook for 10 minutes. Stir in the chicken stock, cover and simmer for 20 minutes more.

Season with the caraway seed, salt, black and cayenne pepper and ketchup. Add the wine. Cover and continue cooking until the meat is tender (about 1 hour more).

Thicken the sauce by adding 2 teaspoons flour mixed with water to the pan. Stir in the mustard, olives and pickle. Cook an additional 5 minutes.

Serves: 6

Spiced Baked Lamb

3 pounds (1½ kilograms) boned lamb shoulder
1 onion, sliced
3 carrots, thinly sliced
3 cloves
1 bay leaf
1 cup vinegar
2 cups water
1 teaspoon salt
½ teaspoon black pepper

1 teaspoon mustard
Oil for frying
1 cup chicken stock
1 tablespoon oil
1 pound (500 grams) potatoes, peeled and sliced
2 tablespoons chives, chopped
½ cup water
1 teaspoon flour

Rinse the meat well and place in a deep bowl. Surround with the onion, carrots, cloves and bay leaf. Pour on the vinegar combined with the water. Cover and refrigerate for 24 hours, turning from time to time.

Dry the meat thoroughly and rub with salt, pepper and mustard. Brown in hot oil on all sides.

Transfer the meat to a baking pan. Add 1 cup chicken stock and the oil. Bake in a medium oven (350°) for about 1½ hours, or until the meat is tender. Baste from time to time.

After about 1 hour, place the potatoes around the meat and baste with the pan juices. When the meat is done, the potatoes should be ready.

Slice the meat and arrange on a platter. Accompany with the sliced potatoes and sprinkle with the chopped chives.

Serve with pan gravy. Strain the pan juices and dilute them with ¼ cup water. Bring to the boil. Add 1 teaspoon flour diluted in ¼ cup water and bring to the boil again, stirring constantly.

Serves: 4-6

Kohlrabi Stuffed with Meat and Avocado

12 kohlrabi roots
½ pound (250 grams) lean beef, ground
1 avocado, mashed
1 slice white bread, soaked in water and squeezed dry
1 teaspoon scallion (shallot), chopped
¼ teaspoon oregano
1 egg
½ teaspoon salt
¼ teaspoon black pepper
3 cups tomato juice
1 teaspoon lemon juice
Avocado balls

Trim the kohlrabi roots, removing the leaves and stems. Scoop out centers of the roots leaving a thin shell of leaves. Combine the meat, avocado, bread, scallion, oregano, egg, salt and pepper and fill the kohlrabi cases with the resulting mixture.

Place the stuffed kohlrabi in a large pot and cook, covered, for 20-30 minutes in the tomato and lemon juices. Garnish with avocado balls.

Serves: 4

Veal with Lima Beans and Artichokes

1 pound (500 grams) breast of veal
3 tablespoons olive oil
1 onion, chopped
2 scallions (shallots), chopped
1 clove garlic, chopped
1 tablespoon parsley, chopped
2 pounds (1 kilogram) fresh lima beans
6 small artichokes
1 teaspoon salt
½ teaspoon black pepper
½ teaspoon oregano
1½-2 cups water

Cut the meat into 2-inch strips. Brown them lightly in oil in a large saucepan. Remove from the pan. Sauté the onion, scallions, garlic, parsley and lima beans in the oil remaining in the pan. Add more oil if necessary. Add the meat to the vegetable mixture.

Remove the tough, outer leaves of the artichokes and cut off the upper third of the remaining leaves. Add to the ingredients in the pan and season with salt, pepper and oregano. Pour in the water and cook over a low flame, stirring occasionally. Add water if needed. When the artichoke leaves pull off easily, the dish is ready to serve.

Serves: 2

Lamb Ribs in Wine

6 cloves garlic, 4 of them chopped
¼ cup parsley
1 teaspoon salt
½ teaspoon black pepper
2 pounds (1 kilogram) ribs of lamb
1½ cups flour

2 eggs, beaten
1 cup oil
½ teaspoon cumin
½ teaspoon saffron
2 cups chicken stock
2 cups dry white wine
Mint leaves

Combine the chopped garlic with 2 tablespoons parsley, ½ teaspoon salt and ¼ teaspoon black pepper. Dip the meat pieces in the resulting mixture then coat them with flour and beaten egg. Fry the ribs in ½ cup oil until golden.

Sauté the remaining garlic and parsley in the rest of the oil. Mix in the cumin, saffron and stock. Add the meat and cook over a medium flame until the cooking liquid evaporates. Add the wine and mint leaves and cook 15 minutes more.

Serves: 6

Lamb with Pomegranate Seeds

2 pomegranates
2 medium onions, finely chopped
1 scallion (shallot), finely chopped

2 tablespoons chives, finely chopped
Salt and black pepper to taste
A 3-pound (1½-kilogram) piece of boned leg of lamb

Remove the seeds from the pomegranates. Combine them with the onions, scallion, and chives, mixing well. Season with salt and pepper.

Line the bottom of a flameproof casserole with half of the pomegranate mixture. Cover with meat and top with the remaining pomegranate mixture. Cover tightly and cook over a medium flame for 10 minutes. Lower the flame and continue cooking for 45 minutes more.

Serves: 6

Lamb with Black-eyed Peas

2 pounds (1 kilogram) black-eyed peas
¼ teaspoon baking soda
1 onion, chopped
2 scallions (shallots), chopped
2 tablespoons oil
1 pound (500 grams) leg of lamb, cut into 1-inch cubes

4 tomatoes, sliced
2 tablespoons green pepper, diced
1 cup chicken stock
1 teaspoon salt
½ teaspoon black pepper
2 tablespoons parsley

Soak the peas and soda in water to cover overnight. Rinse and drain. Sauté the onion and scallions in oil until golden. Add the meat pieces and brown thoroughly. Mix in the black-eyed peas and sauté lightly. Cover the pan and cook over a low flame for 20 minutes. Shake the pan from time to time to prevent the peas from sticking. Do not stir.

After 20 minutes, add the sliced tomatoes, green pepper, chicken stock, salt and pepper. Cook an additional ½ hour over a low flame. Sprinkle with parsley and serve.

Serves: 4-6

Stuffed Lamb

2 cups rice
1 tablespoon salt
1½ teaspoons black pepper
¼ teaspoon cinnamon
½ teaspoon cumin
Pinch of nutmeg
¼ cup raisins

1½ pounds (750 grams) lean beef, ground
5 ounces (150 grams) pine nuts
1 stick (125 grams) margarine
2 tablespoons parsley, chopped
4½ pounds (2 kilograms) shoulder of lamb, boned

Rinse the rice, drain it well and place it in a large pan. Sprinkle with salt, pepper, cinnamon, cumin and nutmeg. Soak the raisins for ½ hour, drain and add to the rice. Combine the ground beef and the pine nuts and sauté in margarine. Mix the meat, nuts and parsley into the rice.

Cut a deep pouch into the lamb shoulder (about half-way through the meat). Fill with the rice and meat mixture. Sew closed.

Place the stuffed shoulder in a flameproof casserole, cover with water and cook until the meat is tender. Transfer the meat to a greased baking pan and bake in a medium oven (350°) until the meat browns. The pan juices may be served as gravy alongside the meat.

Serves: 4

Stuffed Semolina Balls

3 cups semolina
Water
1 pound (500 grams) lean meat
1 small onion
1 scallion (shallot)
½ teaspoon lemon rind, grated
2 tablespoons parsley, chopped

½ teaspoon salt
¼ teaspoon black pepper
¼ teaspoon cardamon
Tomato juice
Worcestershire sauce
1 medium squash, cut into cubes

Add water to the semolina as needed and work into a dough. Reserve.

Put the meat, onion and scallion through the grinder. Transfer to a mixing bowl and add the lemon rind, parsley, salt, pepper and cardamon. Blend thoroughly.

Form the semolina mixture into balls and press a hole into each with your finger. Fill with the meat mixture.

Cook in tomato juice, seasoned with Worcestershire sauce to taste, over a medium flame for 20 minutes. Add the squash cubes to the pan to give additional flavor and color.

Serves: 6

Olives Stuffed with Lamb

1 pound (500 grams) olives
½ pound (250 grams) lean lamb, ground
¼ teaspoon black pepper
1 tablespoon pimiento, minced
1½ cups tomato juice

1 tablespoon oil
Juice of ½ lemon
¼ teaspoon saffron
¼ teaspoon salt
Pinch of cayenne pepper
Pinch of oregano

Make a slit in the olives and carefully remove the pits (stones). Rinse well. Cook the pitted olives in boiling water for 15 minutes. Drain and rinse.

Combine the lamb, black pepper and pimiento, blending thoroughly. Stuff the olives with the prepared mixture. Arrange the stuffed olives in a flame-proof casserole. Add the tomato juice, oil, lemon juice, saffron, salt, cayenne pepper and oregano. Cook over a medium flame until the cooking liquid evaporates. Serve at once.

Serves: 4

Lamb and Eggplant Patties in Tomato Sauce

2 medium eggplants	2 eggs
½ pound (250 grams) lean lamb	½ cup matzo meal
1 large onion	1 tablespoon parsley, chopped
2 scallions (shallots)	½ teaspoon salt
4 anchovy fillets	¼ teaspoon black pepper
5 cloves garlic	2 cups oil for deep-frying

Peel and slice the eggplants. Let them stand in the sun for a while.

Put the eggplant, meat, onion, scallions, anchovy and garlic through the grinder. Add the eggs, matzo meal and parsley. Combine well. Season with salt and pepper and deep-fry in hot oil. Simmer in the prepared sauce (see below) for 30-40 minutes. Serve.

Sauce

8 ripe tomatoes	½ teaspoon salt
1 medium onion, chopped	¼ teaspoon black pepper
3 tablespoons oil	1 teaspoon sugar
1 tablespoon celery, finely diced	3 cups water
2 tablespoons green pepper, finely diced	

Rinse the tomatoes and chop them into large pieces. Sauté the chopped onion in oil in a large saucepan. Add the tomatoes, celery, green pepper, salt, pepper and sugar and cook over a low flame. When the tomatoes have softened, add water and simmer for ½ hour.

Serves: 2

Couscous with Beef Goulash

This dish should be prepared in a steamer (a large double boiler, the top part of which has a perforated bottom). A metal colander, set in a pot with a tightly fitting lid, makes a good substitute.

½ cup chick peas	Pinch of cayenne pepper
¼ teaspoon baking soda	1 teaspoon paprika
1 onion, chopped	6 potatoes, peeled
2 scallions (shallots), chopped	1 pound (500 grams) beef
1½ sticks (180 grams)	(round steak or shinbone), cut
margarine	into 6 pieces
1 tablespoon tomato paste	1 pound (500 grams) semolina
1 teaspoon salt	2 cups water
¼ teaspoon black pepper	

Soak the chick peas and soda overnight in water to cover. Drain.

Sauté the onion and scallions in ½ stick margarine in the bottom half of the steamer. When the vegetables are golden, add the tomato paste, salt, black pepper, cayenne pepper, paprika and a little water.

Let the onion mixture simmer gently while you peel the chick peas and dice the potatoes. Add the chick peas, potatoes and meat to the bottom half of the steamer, cover with water and place the top part of the steamer over the bottom one.

Moisten the semolina with water, drain and place in the upper portion of the steamer. When steam begins to rise from the top of the semolina, add ½ stick margarine and continue steaming for 15 minutes.

Transfer the semolina to a mixing bowl. Add 1 cup water and crumble the resulting mixture by hand. Replace the crumbled semolina in the upper pot. Cook for an additional ½ hour then moisten and crumble again. Return to the pot and continue steaming until tender. The meat should be cooked at the same time.

Arrange the goulash and couscous on a platter and serve at once.

Serves: 4

Liquorish-Flavored Lamb and Quince Ragôut

1 pound (500 grams) leg of lamb, cubed	7 quinces
	Orange juice
Arak (Pernod or anisette may be substituted)	½ teaspoon saffron
	½ teaspoon salt
3 tablespoons oil	¼ teaspoon black pepper
1 cup chicken stock	¼ cup sugar

Marinate the lamb in a little *arak,* Pernod or anisette for 3 hours. Turn from time to time. Drain, dry carefully and sauté in 3 tablespoons oil. Reserve the marinade. Add the chicken stock and simmer for 1 hour.

While the meat is cooking, peel the quinces and soak them in orange juice. Drain, cut into pieces and add to the lamb for the last ½ hour of the cooking period, along with the remaining ingredients. Moisten with marinade and orange juice if necessary.

Serves: 4

Lamb and Chick Pea Ragôut

2 cups chick peas	1 stalk celery, diced
¼ teaspoon baking soda	2 large quinces, peeled and diced
3 cups chicken stock	4 tomatoes, peeled and chopped
1 scallion (shallot), chopped	1 teaspoon salt
1 pound (500 grams) leg of lamb, cubed	½ teaspoon black pepper
	1 tablespoon parsley, chopped
¼ cup oil	

Soak the chick peas and soda overnight in water to cover. Drain and peel. Cook in chicken stock until tender. Drain.

Sauté the scallion and lamb in oil in a frying pan. Add the diced celery and quince. Cook for 5 minutes. Transfer to a large saucepan.

Add the chick peas and chopped tomatoes to the lamb mixture. Season with salt and pepper. Cook for 20 minutes over a medium flame. Sprinkle with parsley and serve at once.

Serves: 4

Lamb with Figs

1 pound (500 grams) figs
1 pound (500 grams) leg of
lamb, cubed
2 onions, chopped
4 scallions (shallots), chopped

2 tablespoons oil
1 teaspoon salt
1 tablespoon chicken stock
2 tablespoons brown sugar

Soak the figs in water for 1 hour. Remove the stems. Chop.

Sauté the lamb, onions and scallions in oil. Brown over a low flame for 10 minutes. Add 1 tablespoon chicken stock and cover. Cook over a low flame for ½ hour, or until tender.

Melt the sugar in a small saucepan. Add to the meat 10 minutes before the end of the cooking period. Stir in the chopped figs. Cook until the pan liquids evaporate.

Serves: 2

Beef Roll Stuffed with Bananas, Dates and Figs

A 2-pound (1-kilogram) piece of
beef, round or flank steak
1 tablespoon mustard
1 teaspoon salt
½ teaspoon black pepper
¼ cup almonds, ground
3 bananas, peeled and sliced

2 cucumber pickles, diced
⅓ cup dates, pitted (stoned)
and chopped
⅓ cup figs, stemmed and
chopped
Oil

Pound the meat until flat. Coat with mustard. Sprinkle with salt, pepper and ground almonds. Cover with sliced bananas, diced pickles, chopped dates and figs.

Roll the meat and fasten with kitchen string. Coat lightly with oil. Wrap the meat roll in aluminum foil.

Place the meat roll in a baking dish and bake in a medium oven (350°) for 1½ hours. Remove from oven, take off the foil and set aside to cool. Slice before serving.

Serves: 4

Beef Balls and Olives

1½ pounds (750 grams) green olives, pitted
3 cups beef stock
6 cloves garlic, chopped
3 tablespoons parsley, chopped
1 pound (500 grams) lean beef, ground

1 tablespoon tomato paste
2 tablespoons onion, minced
½ teaspoon salt
½ teaspoon black pepper
3 tablespoons oil
Cabbage leaves

Cook the olives in boiling water in a large saucepan for 10 minutes. Drain and rinse. Return the olives to the saucepan.

Pour the beef stock over the olives. Add the chopped garlic and 2 tablespoons parsley. Bring to the boil.

Combine the ground beef, tomato paste, onion, salt and black pepper with the remaining parsley. Shape the resulting mixture into small balls. Add to the saucepan with the olives. Stir in the oil. Cook over a medium flame until the cooking liquid evaporates.

Serve hot, garnished with cabbage leaves.

Serves: 4

Brazilian Pot Roast

2 pounds (1 kilogram) rump steak
Juice of 1 lemon
4 slices beef sausage, smoked
1 scallion (shallot), chopped
4 cloves garlic, chopped
1 stalk celery, diced

1 bay leaf
3 tomatoes, peeled and chopped
1 tablespoon salt
½ tablespoon black pepper
1 tablespoon soy sauce
2 cups orange juice

Moisten the meat with lemon juice.

Fry the sausage and remove from the pan. Reserve. Brown the meat in the oil remaining in the frying pan. Transfer to a flameproof casserole. Add the scallion, garlic, celery, bay leaf and tomatoes. Season with salt and pepper. Moisten with soy sauce and orange juice.

Cover and cook over a low flame until the meat is tender (about 2 hours).

Garnish the roast with sausage slices. Cover with the strained sauce. Accompany with boiled potatoes.

Serves: 4

Roast Leg of Lamb with Brown Sauce

1 clove garlic, crushed
½ teaspoon salt
¼ teaspoon cayenne pepper
½ teaspoon mustard
½ teaspoon thyme

3 pounds (1½ kilograms) leg of lamb
½ stick (60 grams) margarine
5 apples, peeled and sliced
1 onion, sliced into rings
3 tomatoes, sliced

Combine the garlic, salt, cayenne pepper, mustard and thyme. Rub into the lamb. Coat the seasoned lamb with ½ of the margarine.

Grease a baking pan with the remaining margarine and add the lamb. Cover with slices of apple, onion and tomato.

Roast in a hot oven (400°) for 20 minutes. Lower the heat to 350° and roast an additional 50 minutes, or until the meat is tender. Accompany with fried rice.

Fried rice

2 cups rice
2 tablespoons oil
½ teaspoon saffron
3 tablespoons soy sauce

1 quart chicken stock
¼ cup pine nuts
2 tablespoons parsley, chopped

Wash and drain the rice.

Heat the oil in a large saucepan. Add the rice and sauté lightly. Add the saffron, soy sauce and chicken stock. Cover and cook 20-25 minutes over a low flame. Stir in the pine nuts and sprinkle with parsley. Serve at once.

Serves: 6

Brains in Tomato Sauce

1 set brains   ¼ teaspoon salt
1 scallion (shallot), chopped   ⅛ teaspoon black pepper
1 tablespoon oil   ⅛ teaspoon nutmeg, grated
½ cup tomato purée   1 teaspoon lemon juice

Soak the brains in cold water for 3 hours. Remove the veins and the outer membranes and dice the brains into medium-sized pieces.

Sauté the scallion in oil. Add the brains, tomato purée, salt, pepper, nutmeg and lemon juice. Cover and cook over a low flame until the brains are tender (10-15 minutes).

Serves: 2

Fennel Logs Stuffed with Calf's Liver

6 large fennel stalks   ½ teaspoon black pepper
1 pound (500 grams) calf's   1 teaspoon lemon juice
liver, chopped   2½ cups water
2 tablespoons parsley, chopped   1 small can tomato paste
1 tablespoon onion, minced   2 tablespoons oil
1 teaspoon salt

Gently hollow out the fennel stalks and cut into 4-inch-long pieces. Rinse, drain and reserve.

Combine the chopped liver, parsley and onion. Blend thoroughly. Season with salt, pepper and lemon juice. Fill the fennel stalks with the resulting mixture.

Put the water, tomato paste and oil in a flameproof casserole. Stir in any remaining liver stuffing. Cook over a medium flame for 15 minutes. Carefully add the stuffed fennel logs to the casserole. Cook over a medium flame for ½ hour, or until the fennel is tender. Moisten with tomato juice, if necessary.

Transfer the fennel logs to a serving dish. Pour on the pan juices. Accompany with boiled rice.

Serves: 6

Sautéed Liver in Tomato Sauce

2 onions, chopped	½ teaspoon salt
2 scallions, chopped	1 small can tomato paste
1 tablespoon oil	½ tablespoon sugar
10 ounces (300 grams) beef liver, cut in pieces	¼ teaspoon black pepper
	1 teaspoon lemon juice
1¼ cups beef stock	1 tablespoon parsley

Sauté the onions and scallions in oil until golden. Add the liver, ¼ cup beef stock and ¼ teaspoon salt. Cook over a low flame for 15 minutes. Mix the tomato paste with the remaining stock and add to the pan. Stir in the sugar, pepper, remaining salt and lemon juice. Cook over a low flame for an additional ½ hour. Sprinkle with parsley and serve at once.

Serves: 3

Calf's Heart and Liver with Mushrooms

10 cloves garlic, crushed	¼ cup green olives, chopped
Pinch of cayenne pepper	½ pound (250 grams) calf's liver, diced
1 tablespoon tomato sauce	
1 teaspoon salt	½ pound (250 grams) calf's heart, diced
1 teaspoon cumin	
½ cup oil	1 small can mushrooms, chopped and drained
½ cup vinegar	
1½ cups beef stock	Chopped parsley

Blend together the garlic, cayenne pepper, tomato sauce, salt and cumin. Cook the resulting mixture in oil for 5 minutes.

Stir in the vinegar and beef stock and continue stirring until well mixed. Add the olives, liver and heart. Simmer for ½ hour.

Add the mushrooms, cook an additional 10 minutes, sprinkle with parsley and serve at once.

Serves: 4

Stuffed Brain Dumpling

1 set calf's brains   Vinegar water

Soak the brains in vinegar for 3 hours. Remove the outer membranes. Cook the brains in fresh vinegar water to cover for about 20 minutes. Do not boil. Drain and slice each brain in half, horizontally. Prepare the filling.

Filling

½ pound (250 grams) lean beef, ground	1 tablespoon chives, finely chopped
1 small can mushrooms, drained and chopped	½ teaspoon salt
3 eggs	¼ teaspoon black pepper
1 tablespoon bread crumbs	¼ teaspoon thyme

Combine the beef, mushrooms, eggs, chives and bread crumbs. Mix well. Season with salt, pepper and thyme. Knead into a dough. Divide the dough into 3 pieces.

To assemble

2 hard-cooked eggs, sliced	1 egg, beaten
Bread crumbs	Oil for frying

Spread a piece of muslin on the table. Place a slice of brain on the muslin and coat it with ⅓ the prepared filling. Cover with ⅓ the egg slices. Top with another slice of brain and repeat the above procedure until all the ingredients have been used, finishing with a slice of brain. Wrap up the stuffed brains securely in the muslin and tie with kitchen string. Cook in boiling water for ½ hour.

Allow the brain dumpling to cool. Remove the cloth, roll the dumpling in bread crumbs, dip in beaten egg and sauté in hot oil until golden. Slice. Prepare the sauce.

Sauce

1 tablespoon water	1 egg yolk
1 clove garlic, crushed	Juice of ½ lemon
2 tablespoons oil	1 tablespoon capers

Boil the water, garlic and oil together in a saucepan. Add the egg yolk, lemon juice and capers. Mix thoroughly.

Serve with the sliced brain dumpling.

Serves: 4

VEGETABLES

Eggplant Stuffed with Lamb

2 pounds (1 kilogram) small eggplants
1 cup lamb, finely diced
1 medium onion, finely chopped
2 scallions (shallots), finely chopped
6 tablespoons oil
1 large tomato, peeled and chopped
1 heaped tablespoon tomato sauce
2 tablespoons unsalted peanuts, roasted, shelled and chopped
½ teaspoon sugar
2 tablespoons parsley, chopped
1 teaspoon salt
¼ teaspoon black pepper
¼ teaspoon rosemary
1 tablespoon oil of hot red peppers (see below)
¾ cup rice

Hollow out the eggplants, making sure to leave the shells intact. Sauté the meat, onion and scallions in 2 tablespoons oil. Remove from flame and add tomato, tomato sauce, peanuts, sugar and parsley. Season with salt, pepper, rosemary and oil of hot red peppers. Blend well. Incorporate the rice and stuff the eggplants with the resulting mixture.

Sauté the stuffed shells gently on all sides in the remaining oil. Arrange side by side in a deep pot. Add water to cover and cook over a low heat until rice is done.

Serves: 4

Oil of Hot Red Peppers

Hot green peppers   Salt
Oil

Hang a string of hot green peppers in the shade for a few weeks. As they dry they will turn red. When they have changed color, take them down and grind them. Place in a jar, salt liberally, and cover with oil. The oil will take on the sharpness of the hot peppers and can be used to season food. Replenish oil as necessary.

Stuffed Artichoke Hearts

3 pounds (1½ kilograms) artichokes
¾ pound (375 grams) margarine
1 pound (500 grams) lean lamb and a piece of lamb fat
1 large onion
3 scallions (shallots)
1 tablespoon salt
1 teaspoon black pepper
1 teaspoon cinnamon
½ teaspoon sage
2 ounces (60 grams) pine nuts

Peel off the artichoke leaves and scoop out the chokes. Soak the artichoke hearts in cold water. Drain. Melt the margarine in a frying pan and sauté the artichoke hearts on all sides. Set aside in a flameproof pot.

Grind the meat, lamb fat, onion and scallions and brown in the margarine remaining in the frying pan. Add salt, pepper, cinnamon, sage and pine nuts. Spoon the meat mixture on to the artichoke hearts, cover with water and cook over a medium flame or bake in a medium oven (350°) until done (about 1 hour).

Serves: 6

Stuffed Onions

3 pounds (1½ kilograms) large onions
¾ cup lean beef, finely chopped
1 egg
1 teaspoon tomato purée
1 teaspoon parsley, chopped
½ teaspoon salt
¼ teaspoon black pepper
½ teaspoon paprika
2 tablespoons dried toast crumbs
4 tablespoons oil
¾ cup water
1 teaspoon cinnamon

Boil the onions for 15 minutes. Drain well and carefully cut a hole in the top of each onion. Gently remove the inner layers and reserve.

Chop the reserved pulp and combine with the meat, egg and tomato purée. Add the parsley, salt, pepper, paprika and toast crumbs. Carefully stuff the onion shells with this mixture and reshape them to close over the openings. Place the onions side by side in a greased baking tin. Moisten with the oil and water and sprinkle with cinnamon. Cover and bake in a medium oven (350°) for 20 minutes.

Serves: 6

Pumpkin Stuffed with Lamb and Raisins

A 5-pound (2½-kilogram) pumpkin
2 pounds (1 kilogram) lean lamb (in one piece)
1 cup oil
1 medium onion, chopped
2 scallions (shallots), chopped
6 cloves garlic, chopped
¾ cup rice, boiled
½ cup raisins
⅓ cup peanuts, chopped
¼ cup parsley, chopped
¼ teaspoon rosemary
½ teaspoon dried mustard
¼ teaspoon cinnamon
A pinch of saffron
1 small can tomato paste
1 cup dry white wine
2 cups water
2 teaspoons lemon juice
1 teaspoon salt
1 tablespoon sugar

Scrape off the thin outer skin of the pumpkin. Cut a circular opening, the size of a water tumbler, in its top. Reserve the cap. Rinse the pumpkin shell well and soak in salted water for 10 minutes.

Set ¾ of the lamb to boil in salted water. Dice the remaining meat and fry in ½ cup oil over a medium flame. Add onion, scallions and garlic and continue cooking, stirring well, for 3 minutes. Incorporate the rice and cook an additional 5 minutes. Remove from flame. Add the raisins, nuts and parsley. Stir in the rosemary, mustard, cinnamon and saffron. Set aside to cool.

Stuff the pumpkin shell with the prepared mixture and replace the cap, securing it in place with string. Pour the remaining oil into a large pot and gently sauté the stuffed shell on all sides. Combine the tomato paste, wine, water, lemon juice, salt and sugar and add to the pot. Cook over a high flame for 10 minutes.

Cover tightly, lower the flame and continue cooking, turning the pumpkin from side to side, until most of the pot liquids are absorbed. When the piece of boiling lamb is sufficiently tender, cut it into strips and add to the pot.

Place the pumpkin on a flat platter, garnish with meat strips and slice horizontally to serve.

Serves: 6-8

Stuffed Celery Stalks

4 large heads of celery
1 pound (500 grams) shoulder
of lamb, in one piece
1 cup oil
2 teaspoons salt
1 teaspoon black pepper
1 pound (500 grams) lean lamb,
ground

1 tablespoon parsley, chopped
2 teaspoons onion, minced
2 eggs
2 tablespoons dried toast
crumbs
1 egg, beaten
Juice of 1 lemon

Wash the celery and remove the leaves. Cut the stalks into 2-inch pieces, reserving the hearts.

Dice the lamb shoulder. Cook gently in a large frying pan, in 4 tablespoons oil, with the celery stalks and half the salt and pepper. While the meat is cooking, trim the reserved celery hearts and cut in ½-inch pieces. Place in a small bowl. Cover with boiling water and let stand 5 minutes. Drain and add to the cooking celery-lamb mixture.

Combine the ground lamb, parsley, minced onion, remaining salt and pepper, 2 eggs, and toast crumbs, working the mixture together well. Fill the celery stalks with the prepared stuffing. Dip in beaten egg. Sauté in ¾ cup oil, first on the stuffed side then on the other. Return the stuffed stalks to the pan with the meat pieces and celery hearts and continue cooking for ½ hour over a low heat. Add the lemon juice and cook an additional hour. Serve with rice.

Serves: 6

Squash Cutlets

2 pounds (1 kilogram) squash
2 eggs
½ cup matzo meal
1 teaspoon onion, minced

¼ teaspoon basil
½ teaspoon salt
¼ teaspoon black pepper
Oil

Peel and grate the squash. Add the remaining ingredients and blend well. Shape into patties and fry in hot oil.

Serves: 6

Eggplant Casserole

½ cup olive oil
1 medium eggplant, peeled and diced
2 green peppers, seeded and diced
3 medium onions, chopped
4 tomatoes, peeled and quartered

¼ cup celery, diced
1 clove garlic, finely chopped
1 bay leaf
1 teaspoon salt
¼ teaspoon black pepper
1 teaspoon sugar

Heat the oil in a heavy casserole. Add the prepared vegetables. Stir in the garlic, bay leaf, salt, pepper and sugar and cook until oil begins to bubble. Lower the flame and simmer over a low heat for 1½ hours.

Serves: 2

Squash Stuffed with Rice and Chick Peas

½ cup chick peas
¼ teaspoon baking soda
2 pounds (1 kilogram) squash
1 large onion, sliced
4 tablespoons oil
2 tomatoes
1½ cups rice

1 tablespoon parsley, chopped
1 teaspoon Worcestershire sauce
¼ teaspoon oregano
½ teaspoon salt
¼ teaspoon black pepper

Soak the chick peas and soda overnight in water to cover. Rinse well. Drain. Cut the squashes in half, horizontally, hollow them out and chop half the removed pulp, discarding the rest.

Sauté the chopped onion in 2 tablespoons oil until golden. Drain. Purée the tomatoes and combine with the rice, parsley, Worcestershire sauce, oregano, salt and pepper. Incorporate the sautéed onion and chopped squash pulp.

Fill the squash cases ¾ full. Sauté gently in the remaining oil. Place the filled cases in a large pot and cover with water. Bring to a boil. Lower flame and cook over low heat for 3 hours.

Serves: 6

Stuffed Squash in Tomato Sauce

2 pounds (1 kilogram) small squash	1 small can tomato paste
	Boiling water
1 medium onion, chopped	½ teaspoon salt
2 scallions (shallots), chopped	¼ teaspoon black pepper
1 tablespoon oil	½ teaspoon paprika
1 cup rice	½ teaspoon basil
¼ cup chicken liver, chopped	1 tablespoon margarine
1 cup beef, ground	1 teaspoon flour
1 teaspoon chicken fat	½ cup water

Cut squashes in half and hollow out the insides. Reserve the shells. Sauté the onion and scallions in oil and mix into the rice. Combine the chopped chicken liver, ground beef and chicken fat. Incorporate into the rice mixture. Season.

Lightly sauté the squash shells in oil. Fill them with the prepared filling and place them in a deep frying pan. Cover with tomato paste and boiling water. Sprinkle with salt, pepper, paprika and basil. Cook over a low heat until the rice has absorbed all the liquid.

Heat the margarine in a small saucepan, stir in the flour and add the water. Spread the resulting mixture over the squash. Continue cooking for 15 minutes.

Serves: 6

Eggplant Patties

1 eggplant	½ teaspoon salt
2 scallions (shallots)	¼ teaspoon black pepper
1 tablespoon oil	1 clove garlic, crushed
2 tablespoons lean lamb, ground	1 tablespoon parsley
7 teaspoons matzo meal	Oil for frying
1 egg	

Boil the unpeeled eggplant in water for 20 minutes, or until soft. Set aside. When the eggplant has cooled, squeeze out the water. Peel and mash the eggplant. Reserve.

Sauté the scallions in oil and add to the ground lamb. Put the meat mixture and the eggplant through the grinder. Add matzo meal, egg, salt, pepper, garlic and parsley. Mix well. Form into patties and fry in hot oil.

Serves: 2

Stuffed Brandy Squash in Wine Sauce

6 medium sized squashes
¼ cup onion, chopped
2 tablespoons oil
¼ teaspoon salt
⅛ teaspoon black pepper
2 cups lean beef, ground
1 teaspoon garlic, crushed

1 teaspoon Parmesan cheese, grated
2 tablespoons mint leaves, crushed
1 teaspoon sugar
2 tablespoons brandy
2 tablespoons lemon juice
2 tablespoons water

Cut squashes in half, horizontally, and hollow them out. Soak the squash cases in salted water for 15 minutes. Rinse well.

Sauté the onion in oil with the salt and pepper until golden. Combine the meat, garlic, cheese, mint and sugar and add to the onions. Moisten with brandy, lemon juice and water.

Cook over a low flame, stirring constantly, until the liquids have almost evaporated. Fill the squash cases with the resulting mixture and place side by side in a large, lidded, flameproof casserole. Cover with sauce.

Sauce

½ cup lemon juice
1 tablespoon sugar
1 tablespoon tomato paste
¼ cup red wine

1½ cups water
¼ cup olive oil
1 bay leaf

Combine the above ingredients and pour over the filled squashes. Cover and cook over a high flame until ⅔ of the sauce if absorbed. Lower the heat and continue cooking until the remaining liquid has disappeared.

Serves: 6

Eggplant Casserole

1 large eggplant
1-2 tablespoons mustard
½ teaspoon salt
⅛ teaspoon black pepper
Pinch of cayenne pepper
1 tablespoon margarine
1 large onion, sliced
1 large tomato, sliced
1 green pepper, seeded and diced
1 stalk fennel, diced

Cut the unpeeled eggplant into thin slices. Coat lightly with mustard. Sprinkle with salt, black pepper and cayenne pepper.

Grease a glass baking dish with margarine. Arrange the prepared vegetables in layers: first ½ the eggplant, then a layer of onion slices, next a combined layer of tomato, pepper and fennel. Top with the remaining eggplant. Cover and bake in a medium oven (350°) until vegetables are soft (about ½ hour).

Serves: 2

Eggplant with Cheese

3 small eggplants
1½ teaspoons salt
¾ cup flour
3 tablespoons margarine or oil
1 medium onion, chopped
2 scallions (shallots), chopped
2 cups tomato purée
1 teaspoon lemon juice
1½ cups water
¼ teaspoon black pepper
¼ teaspoon basil
1 clove garlic, crushed
1 cup Parmesan cheese, grated

Peel the eggplants and cut into ½-inch-thick slices. Sprinkle with 1 teaspoon salt. Coat with flour and sauté in margarine or oil. Drain on paper towels.

Sauté the onion and scallions in oil. Combine the tomato purée, lemon juice and water and add to the onion mixture. Simmer for a moment or two. Add the remaining salt, pepper, basil and crushed garlic. Simmer 5 minutes. Remove from heat.

Arrange the eggplant slices in a greased baking tin. Cover with the tomato mixture and sprinkle with grated cheese. Bake in a medium oven (350°) for 20 minutes.

Serves: 6

Stuffed Eggplants

2 pounds (1 kilogram) small eggplants
1 medium onion
2 scallions (shallots)
2 tablespoons oil
3 cloves garlic, chopped
¼ cup parsley, chopped
½ cup water
2 slices white bread, soaked in water and squeezed dry

2 eggs, beaten
1 teaspoon strong chicken stock
½ teaspoon salt
¼ teaspoon black pepper
¼ teaspoon oregano
1 cup flour
Oil for frying.

Scrape off the outer skins of the eggplants. Cut them in half, horizontally, and scoop out the insides. Chop the eggplant pulp.

Sauté the onion and scallions in oil. Add the eggplant pulp, garlic, parsley and water. Cover. Lower the flame. When the water in the pan has evaporated, press on the resulting mixture with a fork to extract any remaining liquid. Add the bread to the pan and mash into the eggplant mixture with a fork. Cook until the contents of the pan are completely dry. Remove from heat. Transfer to a mixing bowl.

Add one of the beaten eggs, the chicken stock, salt, pepper and oregano to the eggplant mixture and combine well. Fill the prepared cases with this stuffing. Dip the open face of the stuffed shells first in flour then in the remaining egg and fry in oil. Reserve any oil remaining in the pan. Transfer the eggplants to a deep saucepan. Prepare the sauce.

Sauce

1 clove garlic, chopped
1 cup tomato juice or 4 medium tomatoes, peeled and chopped
½ teaspoon salt

½ cup water
2 teaspoons strong chicken stock
Cayenne pepper to taste (optional)

Sauté the chopped garlic in the reserved frying oil. Add tomato juice (or fresh tomatoes) and salt. Simmer for a few minutes then pour the sauce over the eggplant. Add water and chicken stock. Cook for ½ hour until water evaporates and sauce thickens. Season with cayenne pepper (optional).

Serves: 4

Eggplant Stuffed with Cheese

6 medium eggplants   1 tablespoon margarine
Salted water

Cut the eggplants in half, horizontally, and cook in salted water for 10 minutes. Drain and set aside.

When the eggplants have cooled, hollow them out with a spoon. Chop and reserve the pulp. Arrange the eggplant cases in a large baking dish, greased with margarine. Stuff with the prepared filling and bake in a medium oven (350°) for ½-¾ hour.

Filling

3 eggs
½ teaspoon salt
⅛ teaspoon black pepper
⅛ teaspoon nutmeg

1 teaspoon chives, finely chopped
3 ounces (90 grams) Mozzarella cheese
¼ cup Gouda cheese, grated

Beat eggs well and incorporate the reserved eggplant pulp, salt, pepper, nutmeg and chives. Add the cheeses and blend thoroughly.

Serves: 6

Stuffed Potato Pancakes

1 pound (500 grams) potatoes
1 teaspoon saffron
1 hard-cooked egg
½ cup lean lamb (or beef), diced
1 tablespoon onion, minced
1 teaspoon tomato purée

1 tablespoon parsley, finely chopped
¼ teaspoon salt
½ teaspoon black pepper
¼ cup flour
Oil for frying

Cook and mash the potatoes well. Add the saffron and divide the mixture into 8 parts.

Grind the egg and meat together, add the onion, tomato purée and parsley and blend thoroughly. Season with salt and pepper. Divide into 8 portions. Coat each portion of the meat mixture with a blanket of mashed potatoes. Dip in flour and fry in hot oil.

Serves: 8

Baked Eggplant with Potatoes

1½ pounds (750 grams) potatoes (unpeeled)
1 pound (500 grams) eggplant
1½ teaspoons salt
1 teaspoon mustard
1 cup cream
4 tablespoons margarine
1 medium onion, chopped

¼ cup green pepper, finely diced
¼ teaspoon black pepper
¼ teaspoon oregano
1 teaspoon vinegar
3 eggs, hard-cooked
10 ounces (300 grams) Gouda cheese, diced

Boil the potatoes in their jackets. Cool, peel and slice.

Slice the eggplant and sprinkle with 1 teaspoon salt. Set aside to drain. Combine the mustard and cream. Reserve.

Thoroughly rinse the drained eggplant slices. Sauté in 3 tablespoons margarine with the chopped onion, green pepper, remaining salt, black pepper and oregano. Add vinegar and continue to cook for 2 minutes. Remove from heat.

Peel and slice the eggs.

Grease a baking dish with the remaining margarine and line with ½ the potatoes. Coat with ⅓ cup cream, top with ½ the eggplant-onion-pepper mixture, cover with another ⅓ cup cream. Add a layer of egg slices, the remaining potatoes, the rest of the cream and finish off with the remaining eggplant. Sprinkle with diced cheese. Bake in a medium oven (350°) for 15 minutes. Increase heat to 400° and bake an additional 30 minutes. Serve hot.

Serves: 4

Spinach Pie

Dough:

1 cup water   ½ teaspoon salt
2 ounces (60 grams) margarine   4 eggs
½ cup flour

Boil the water and margarine. Add the flour, stirring constantly, and bring to the boil again. Continue to cook and stir for 5 minutes. Set aside to cool. Add the eggs and blend well. Roll and place in a greased, deep-dish pie plate. Prick. Bake in a medium oven (350°) for about 15 minutes. Reserve.

Filling:

1 onion, chopped   ½ teaspoon salt
2 tablespoons margarine   ¼ teaspoon pepper
1 pound (500 grams) fresh   ⅛ teaspoon nutmeg
spinach, chopped   1 teaspoon sugar
½ cup chicken stock

Sauté the onion in margarine until golden. Add the spinach and chicken stock and cook over a medium flame until spinach is done. Drain well. Season with salt, pepper, nutmeg and sugar. Just before serving, warm the spinach mixture and fill the prepared pie crust. Place in a medium oven (350°) until crust has heated through. Serve at once.

Serves: 4

Stuffed Tomatoes

1 package fish fillets   2 gherkins, diced
2 tablespoons lime juice   ¼ teaspoon mustard
½ teaspoon salt   4 tablespoons mayonnaise
1 cup peas, cooked   8 tomatoes

Poach the fillets in water to cover with the lime juice and salt. Let cool, drain and chop. Add the peas, gherkins, mustard and mayonnaise. Mix thoroughly. Hollow out the tomatoes. Fill the tomato cases with the prepared fish mixture.

Serves: 6

Stuffed Leeks

2 pounds (1 kilogram) leeks	1½ teaspoons salt
1 pound (500 grams) lean beef, chopped	¾ teaspoon black pepper
	1½ cups oil
3 slices melba toast	1 teaspoon saffron
2 scallions (shallots)	1 teaspoon thyme
4 eggs, 2 whole and 2 beaten separately	2 tablespoons lemon juice

Soak the leeks in water for ½ hour. Rinse well and cook in salted water for 1 hour. Drain, reserving 1 cup of the cooking liquid.

Put the meat, toast and scallions through the grinder. Add 2 whole eggs, ½ teaspoon salt and ¼ teaspoon pepper. Blend well. Trim off the green portion of the leeks and reserve. Slit the white part of the leeks and stuff with some of the prepared meat mixture. Dip the stuffed leeks in a beaten egg and fry in ¾ cup oil.

Put the green portion of the leeks through a food mill. Combine with the remaining meat mixture, blending thoroughly. Add the remaining beaten egg, ½ teaspoon salt and ¼ teaspoon pepper. Mix well, shape into patties and fry in the remaining oil.

Add the remaining salt and pepper, the saffron, thyme and lemon juice to the reserve cup of cooking liquid. Pour into a flameproof casserole. Add the stuffed leeks and leek patties. Cook over a low flame for ½ hour.

Serves: 4

Filled Eggplant Quarters

2 eggplants
½ pound (500 grams) lean
lamb, ground
2 scallions (shallots), chopped
3 tablespoons matzo meal
2 eggs, beaten
2 tablespoons green olives,
chopped

2 tablespoons celery, chopped
1 teaspoon salt
¼ teaspoon black pepper
1 small can tomato paste
3 cups water
1 teaspoon lemon juice
½ teaspoon paprika

Cut the eggplants into quarters, lengthwise. Make a slit lengthwise and a slit crosswise on the inner surface of each eggplant quarter.

Place the lamb in a mixing bowl. Add the scallions, matzo meal, eggs, olives and celery. Combine well. Season with salt and pepper. Spread the resulting mixture over the slit sides of the eggplant quarters.

Arrange the eggplant in a flameproof casserole. Combine the tomato paste, water, lemon juice and paprika. Add the tomato sauce to the casserole and simmer over a low flame for ½ hour or until the eggplant is tender.

Serves: 8

Cabbage Leaves Stuffed with Rice and Currants

2 pounds (1 kilogram) cabbage
1 cup rice
2½ cups salted water
¼ cup currants
2 tablespoons pine nuts

1 teaspoon cinnamon
¾ cup sugar plus 1 tablespoon
Juice of ½ lemon
2 sticks (250 grams) margarine,
softened

Steam the cabbage leaves until soft. Cook rice in salted water until half done (about 10 minutes). Combine the currants, pine nuts, ½ teaspoon cinnamon, ¾ cup sugar, lemon juice and ½ the margarine. Fill the cabbage leaves with this mixture and roll closed.

Melt the remaining margarine in a large saucepan with the remaining cinnamon and 1 tablespoon sugar. Add the stuffed cabbage leaves. Cook over a low heat for 1¼ hours. Serve hot.

Serves: 4

Stuffed Squash and Quince

2 pounds (1 kilogram) squash
½ cup rice
½ cup lean lamb, ground
1 teaspoon salt
¼ teaspoon black pepper
½ teaspoon cinnamon

⅛ teaspoon cloves, ground
3 tablespoons oil
1 pound (500 grams) large, whole quinces
¾ cup lime juice

Wash the squashes, cut them in half horizontally, and gently remove the insides.

Combine the rice and meat. Mix in ½ teaspoon salt, the pepper, cinnamon and cloves and add 1 tablespoon oil. Half-fill the squash cases with the prepared mixture.

Wash the quinces. Peel and cut into cubes. Place in a deep, flameproof casserole with the remaining oil. Add the stuffed squash. Cover with water, combined with the lime juice and remaining salt. Bring to the boil. Lower the flame and cook until almost all the water has evaporated.

Serves: 4

Baked Avocado Stuffed with Salmon

3 large avocados
1 tablespoon lemon juice
1 teaspoon salt
4 tablespoons margarine
6 tablespoons flour
1½ cups milk
¼ teaspoon black pepper

2 tablespoons pimientos, chopped
½ cup green peas, cooked
1½ cups salmon, chopped
1 onion, minced
3 gherkins, chopped
¼ cup celery, chopped
⅔ cup Gouda cheese, grated

Cut the avocados in half, lengthwise. Remove the stones. Sprinkle the avocado halves with lemon juice and ½ teaspoon salt. Reserve.

Melt the margarine in a large saucepan. Stir in the flour, blend thoroughly and add the milk, stirring constantly. Continue cooking and stirring until the sauce thickens. Season with the remaining salt and the pepper. Add the pimientos, peas, salmon, onion, gherkins and celery. Mix well.

Fill the avocado halves with the prepared stuffing. Sprinkle with grated cheese. Place the stuffed avocados in a baking pan. Fill the pan about 1-inch full of water. Bake in a medium oven (350°) for 15 minutes.

Serves: 6

Sweet Potatoes Stuffed with Spinach

½ pound (250 grams) fresh spinach
3 large sweet potatoes
1 tablespoon margarine
1 small onion, chopped
¼ cup chicken stock
⅛ teaspoon nutmeg

1 egg
½ teaspoon salt
¼ teaspoon black pepper
2 tablespoons matzo meal
Oil for frying
1 can tomato sauce

Rinse the spinach, remove the stems and drain. Reserve.

Parboil the potatoes for 5 minutes. Peel and slice in half, lengthwise. Scoop out the centers. Reserve the cases.

Put 1 tablespoon margarine in a large saucepan. When it begins to bubble, add the onion and sauté. Add the reserved spinach and ¼ cup chicken stock. Cook until the spinach is limp (about 5 minutes). Stir in nutmeg.

Remove the spinach, drain and chop. Stir in the egg, salt, pepper and matzo meal. Fill the potato cases with the resulting mixture.

Heat oil in a flameproof casserole. Add the stuffed potatoes and sauté until the cases are cooked and crusty. Transfer to a serving dish. Heat the tomato sauce in a small saucepan, spoon over the spinach and serve at once.

Serves: 6

Potato Dough

1 pound (500 grams) potatoes
1 tablespoon salt
2 ounces (60 grams) margarine
¼ cup milk
¾ cup flour
2 eggs, beaten

1 teaspoon parsley, finely chopped
¼ teaspoon ginger
¼ teaspoon black pepper
⅛ teaspoon nutmeg

Peel and dice the potatoes. Cook in boiling water until tender. Drain and mash. Season with salt.

Add the margarine and milk, mixing well. Stir in the flour and beaten eggs and knead the resulting mixture into a smooth dough. Incorporate the parsley. Season with ginger, pepper and nutmeg.

This versatile dough may be filled with a variety of ingredients including spinach, mushrooms, chopped onions and peppers, cheese, etc.

Vegetable and Rice Pie

1 cup rice	2 eggs, separated
3½ cups chicken stock	1 teaspoon salt
½ cup sweet red peppers, seeded and diced	¼ teaspoon black pepper
2 tablespoons margarine	⅛ teaspoon thyme
1 8-ounce (250-gram) can corn kernels, drained	2 tablespoons parsley, finely chopped
1 8-ounce (250-gram) can peas and carrots, drained	Bread crumbs
	1 tablespoon mustard

Cook the rice in 2½ cups chicken stock until tender (about 20 minutes).

Sauté the red peppers in margarine until soft.

Combine the rice, red peppers, corn and peas and carrots. Stir in the egg yolks and season with ½ teaspoon salt, the black pepper, the thyme and the parsley. Moisten with the remaining chicken stock.

Grease a baking dish and sprinkle it with bread crumbs. Add the rice mixture. Bake in a medium oven (350°) for ½ hour.

While the pie is baking, whip the egg whites until stiff. Add the mustard and the remaining salt. Combine gently. At the end of the baking period, remove the pie from the oven and cover it with beaten egg white. Return to the oven for an additional 15 minutes, or until the crust is golden. Serve at once.

Serves: 4

Baked Eggplant Pie

1 large eggplant
1 teaspoon salt
3 potatoes
1 teaspoon mustard
1 cup cream
1 cup Gouda cheese, grated
1 teaspoon onion, minced

½ cup Feta cheese, crumbled
3 eggs, hard-cooked and sliced
½ cup stuffed green olives, sliced
2 eggs, beaten
½ teaspoon nutmeg

Peel and slice the eggplant. Salt the slices and set them aside.

Boil the potatoes in their jackets. When they are cooked, peel and slice.

Combine the mustard with the cream, mixing well.

Place the eggplant slices in a greased baking dish. Cover with ½ of the cream sauce. Sprinkle with ½ the grated cheese. Add a layer of sliced potatoes, sprinkle with the minced onion and cover with the remaining cream sauce. Top with Feta cheese. Decorate with slices of hard-cooked egg and the sliced olives.

Pour the beaten eggs over the pie. Sprinkle with the remaining grated cheese and nutmeg. Bake in a medium oven (350°) until the cheese forms a golden crust (about ½ hour).

Serves: 6

Eggplant and Pimiento Pie

2 large eggplants
1 teaspoon salt
Juice of 1 lemon
6 pimientos, finely chopped
½ cup pine nuts

2 tablespoons parsley, chopped
2 cups prepared *tehina* (for preparation, see page 20)
Lettuce leaves

Peel the eggplants and grate them coarsely. Place in a large mixing bowl and season with salt and lemon juice. Stir in the pimientos, pine nuts and parsley. Mix thoroughly.

Place 1 cup prepared *tehina* in a baking dish. Cover with the eggplant mixture. Top with the remaining *tehina*.

Bake in a medium oven (350°) for 40 minutes. Spoon onto lettuce leaves and serve at once.

Serves: 4

Baked Squash Stuffed with Mushrooms

3 pounds (1½ kilograms) summer squash
Oil for frying
½ pound (250 grams) fresh mushrooms
2 ounces (60 grams) margarine
1 scallion (shallot), chopped
¼ cup parsley, chopped
½ teaspoon salt
2 tablespoons almonds, blanched and chopped

Cut the squash in half, horizontally, and scoop out the pulp, leaving a ½-inch shell. Reserve the pulp.

Sauté the squash cases lightly in oil on all sides. Place in a greased baking pan.

Wash and chop the mushrooms. Sauté in margarine with the scallion, reserved squash pulp, parsley and salt. Stir in the almonds and blend thoroughly. Fill the squash cases with the resulting mixture.

Prepare the sauce.

Sauce

2 cans condensed cream of mushroom soup
1½ cups milk
4 eggs
1 tablespoon margarine, softened
⅛ teaspoon ginger
⅛ teaspoon nutmeg
2 tablespoons sherry
¼ cup Parmesan cheese, grated

Dilute the soup with milk over a low flame. Beat in the eggs and margarine, stirring constantly. Season with ginger and nutmeg. Add the sherry.

Spoon the prepared sauce over the stuffed squash, sprinkle with grated cheese and bake in a medium oven (350°) for 45 minutes.

Serves: 6

Zucchini Stuffed with Chicken and Walnuts

2 pounds (1 kilogram) zucchini (squash)
2½ teaspoons salt
3 chicken breasts, boned
2 slices white bread
10 cloves garlic
½ cup walnuts, shelled
1 tablespoon parsley, chopped
1 tablespoon celery, finely chopped
¼ teaspoon black pepper
¼ teaspoon saffron
3 tablespoons oil
2 eggs, beaten
1 cup flour
Oil for frying

Cut the zucchini in half, lengthwise. Carefully scoop out the insides and sprinkle the cases with 1½ teaspoons salt. Let stand for 10 minutes.

Put the chicken, bread, garlic and walnuts through the grinder. Add the parsley, celery, remaining salt, pepper and saffron. Combine thoroughly, moistening with 3 tablespoons oil. Fill the zucchini cases with the resulting mixture.

Dip the stuffed zucchini first in beaten egg then in flour. Sauté gently in hot oil on all sides.

Arrange the sautéed zucchini in a greased baking dish. Bake in a medium oven (350°) for 45 minutes.

Serves: 4

Artichokes Stuffed with Cheese

6 artichokes
1 cup Ricotta cheese
1 cup Parmesan cheese, grated
2 tablespoons anchovies, chopped
2 tablespoons celery, chopped
¼ teaspoon black pepper
Pinch of nutmeg
Bread crumbs
1 egg, beaten
Paprika

Arrange the artichokes in a large stew pot. Cover with water. Slowly bring to the boil. When the water begins boiling, drain it off. After the artichokes have cooled slightly, remove their stems, chokes and tough outer leaves.

Combine the cheeses, anchovies and celery. Season with pepper and nutmeg. Mix in the bread crumbs and beaten egg. Blend thoroughly.

Fill the artichoke cases with the prepared mixture, sprinkle with paprika and bake in a medium oven (350°) for 15 minutes.

Serves: 6

Eggplant Stuffed with Curried Eggs

6 medium eggplants
1 onion, chopped
2 scallions (shallots), chopped
Oil for frying
4 eggs, 2 of them hard-cooked
3 cloves garlic
¼ cup almonds, blanched

2 tablespoons soybean flour
1 tablespoon parsley, chopped
1 teaspoon salt
½ teaspoon black pepper
¼ teaspoon cumin
Curry powder to taste
2 cups tomato juice

Rinse the eggplants and cut them in half. Scoop out the pulp and steam it in a metal colander set over a saucepan of boiling water. Reserve the eggplant cases.

Sauté the onion and scallions in oil until golden.

Put the eggplant pulp, onion, scallions, hard-cooked eggs, garlic and almonds through the grinder. Add the remaining eggs, the soybean flour and the parsley. Combine thoroughly and season with salt, pepper, cumin and curry powder.

Stuff the curried egg mixture into the eggplant cases.

Arrange the stuffed eggplants in a flameproof casserole. Bake in a medium oven (350°) until the eggplant cases have softened. Remove from the oven, pour in the tomato juice and cook over a medium flame, adding more tomato juice if necessary, until the sauce thickens and the eggplants are cooked.

Serves: 6

Tomatoes Stuffed with Eggplant

1 pound (500 grams) eggplant
2 eggs, hard-cooked
1 slice white bread, soaked in
water and squeezed dry
½ teaspoon salt

¼ teaspoon black pepper
1 tablespoon parsley, chopped
2 scallions (shallots), chopped
1 teaspoon lime juice
8 tomatoes

Cook the unpeeled eggplant in boiling water until tender. Peel and put the pulp through the grinder with the eggs and bread. Place in a mixing bowl and season with salt and pepper. Stir in the parsley, chopped scallions and lime juice and blend thoroughly.

Hollow out the tomatoes, being careful not to puncture the skins. Fill the tomato cases with the eggplant mixture.

Serves: 8

Stuffed Red Peppers in Cheese Sauce

12 large sweet red peppers	3 eggs, hard-cooked
1½ pounds (750 grams) eggplant	4 anchovy fillets
3 teaspoons salt	1 tablespoon parsley, chopped
2 onions, sliced into rings	½ teaspoon black pepper
Oil	½ teaspoon ginger

Remove the tops from the peppers. Scoop out the seeds and remove the membranes. Rinse and drain. Reserve the red pepper cases.

Peel the eggplants and slice them into ½-inch-thick rounds. Sprinkle with 2 teaspoons salt and set aside.

Coat with the prepared onion rings. Bake in a medium oven (350°) for 10 minutes, turning once. Set aside to cool.

Put the eggplant, onions, 2 eggs and anchovies through the grinder. Add the parsley and season with the remaining salt, the pepper and a pinch of ginger. Stuff the reserved pepper cases with the prepared filling. Coat the cases with oil. Arrange in a baking pan. Grate the remaining hard-cooked egg and sprinkle it over the peppers. Bake in a medium oven (350°) for 20 minutes. Prepare the vegetable garnish.

Vegetable Garnish

2 pounds (1 kilogram) yellow or green beans	1 slice stale bread
2 pounds (1 kilogram) cauliflower	2 teaspoons salt

Rinse and string the beans. Rinse and trim the cauliflower. Divide into florets.

Place the beans and cauliflower in a stew pot. Add the stale bread (to absorb the cooking odors) and 2 teaspoons salt. Fill the pot halfway with water. Cook until the vegetables are tender. Drain. Place the cauliflower in one dish and the beans in another. Prepare the sauce.

Cheese Sauce

¼ pound (125 grams) Gouda cheese	2 tablespoons corn oil
1 cup plain yogurt	1 teaspoon honey
	3 gherkins

2 tablespoons lemon juice   1 teaspoon cumin
5 cloves garlic   ½ teaspoon black pepper
1 teaspoon mustard   1 teaspoon salt
2 tablespoons chives, chopped

Place the above ingredients in a blender. Blend until smooth.

To assemble

½ pound (250 grams) avocado   Lettuce leaves
Lemon juice   Tangerine sections

Divide the cheese sauce in half. Mix ½ with the cauliflower and the rest with the beans.

Peel the avocado. Sprinkle with lemon juice. Slice.

Rinse and drain the lettuce leaves.

Arrange the stuffed peppers on a bed of lettuce leaves. Garnish with mounds of vegetables, avocado slices and tangerine sections.

Serves: 12

Mashed Potato and Onion Pie

½ pound (250 grams) onions, chopped   3 eggs, separated
7 tablespoons margarine   1 teaspoon salt
2 pounds (1 kilogram) potatoes   ½ teaspoon black pepper
½ cup milk   Nutmeg
Chopped chives

Sauté the chopped onions in 3 tablespoons margarine until golden. Reserve. Peel, boil and drain the potatoes. Put them through a dicer while they are still hot. Slowly add the milk (brought to the boil), stirring constantly. When the mixture is well blended, add the remaining margarine, the egg yolks and the reserved onions. Combine well.

Whip the egg whites and fold them carefully into the potato mixture. Season with salt, pepper and nutmeg to taste.

Transfer the potato and onion to a greased baking dish. Brown in a hot oven (400°). Sprinkle with chopped chives before serving.

Serves: 8

Sweet Potato, Chicken and Vegetable Pancake

2 pounds (1 kilogram) sweet potatoes
8 eggs, 2 of them hard-cooked
1 cup chicken, diced
Dash of Worcestershire sauce
3 tablespoons parsley, chopped
1 teaspoon salt
1 teaspoon saffron

½ teaspoon black pepper
2 carrots, cooked and diced
1 small can mushrooms, drained and chopped
2 pimientos, chopped
¾ cup oil for frying
Paprika

Boil the potatoes in their jackets until tender. Drain, peel and mash.

Beat the 6 uncooked eggs. Add the chicken, Worcestershire, parsley, salt, saffron and black pepper. Stir into the mashed potatoes. Blend thoroughly.

Chop the 2 hard-cooked eggs. Combine with the carrots, mushrooms and pimientos. Add to the potato and egg. Mix well.

Heat ½ cup oil in a skillet. Add the prepared mixture and cover. Cook over a very low flame for ½ hour, or until the underside of the pancake is brown. Turn the pancake out onto a plate, heat the remaining oil in the skillet and brown the patty on its uncooked side for an additional 10 minutes.

Sprinkle with paprika. Serve at once.

Serves: 4

Squash Patties Amandine

2 squashes, cooked
5 ounces (150 grams) almonds, blanched and slivered
¼ cup figs, finely chopped
½ cup brown sugar
½ cup bread crumbs
1 teaspoon lemon peel, grated

2 eggs
½ teaspoon almond extract
1 teaspoon baking powder
1 stick (125 grams) margarine, melted
Crushed pineapple

Mash and drain the squash pulp. Mix in the almonds, figs, brown sugar, bread crumbs and lemon peel. Blend thoroughly. Beat in the eggs, add the almond extract, baking powder and ½ the margarine and combine well. Shape the squash mixture into patties.

Heat the remaining margarine in a frying pan and cook the patties on both sides over a low flame.

Sprinkle with crushed pineapple. Serve at once.

Serves: 4

Squash Stuffed with Cheese and Raisins

9 summer squash
1 cup rice, rinsed and drained
3 ounces (90 grams) Feta cheese
3 ounces (90 grams) Mozzarella cheese
5 tablespoons tomato paste
1 tablespoon scallion (shallot), minced
1 tablespoon parsley, chopped
¼ cup raisins
3 pimientos, chopped
1 egg
½ teaspoon salt
¼ teaspoon black pepper
2 cups water
Lemon juice
Sugar

Rinse the squashes and lightly scrape their peels. Slice each squash in half, lengthwise. Scoop out the pulp. Reserve the cases.

Place the rice in a mixing bowl. Add the Feta and Mozzarella cheese, 2 tablespoons tomato paste, the scallion, parsley, raisins, pimientos and egg. Season with salt and pepper. Combine thoroughly. Fill the squash cases with the cheese and raisin mixture.

Arrange the stuffed squashes in a flameproof casserole. Dilute the remaining tomato paste in 2 cups water. Pour over the squash. Cook over a low flame for 1½ hours. Before serving, stir lemon juice and sugar to taste into the sauce.

Serves: 6

Stuffed Squash in Yogurt Sauce

8 summer squashes
½ cup rice, boiled
¼ cup Feta cheese
2 pimientos, chopped
3 gherkins, chopped
1½ tablespoons oil
¼ teaspoon salt
¼ teaspoon black pepper
3 cloves garlic
1½ tablespoons mint leaves
3 cups plain yogurt

Rinse the squashes, scrape their peels lightly and cut them in half. Remove and discard the pulpy centers.

Combine the rice, cheese, pimientos, gherkins, oil, salt and pepper in a mixing bowl. Blend thoroughly and spoon into the squash cases.

Place the stuffed squashes in a deep, flameproof casserole. Cover with water. Mash together the garlic and mint leaves and add to the pan. Cook over a medium flame until ½ of the water has evaporated. Add the yogurt. Lower the flame and continue cooking until the yogurt thickens like cream. Serve cold.

Serves: 8

Cauliflower and Pear Pie

1 large cauliflower
3 firm pears
3 eggs, beaten
1 teaspoon salt
½ teaspoon black pepper
Pinch of nutmeg
3 tablespoons bread crumbs

2 sweet red peppers, seeded
and cut into strips
5 black olives, pitted and sliced
1 small can mushrooms, drained
and sliced
1 teaspoon onion, minced
1 tablespoon parsley, chopped

Clean and trim the cauliflower. Drop into boiling water, add the pears and cook until tender. Drain.

Put the cauliflower and pears through the grinder. Add the beaten eggs, salt, pepper, nutmeg and bread crumbs. Blend thoroughly.

Put ¼ of the cauliflower mixture in a greased baking tin. Cover with ⅓ of the red pepper strips and olive slices. Add another ¼ of the cauliflower. Top with the mushrooms combined with the minced onion. Add another ¼ of the cauliflower and cover with ½ the remaining red pepper and olive slices, reserving the rest. Finish with the remaining cauliflower.

Place the pie in the oven and bake at medium heat (350°) until the top is golden (about 40 minutes).

Before serving, sprinkle with chopped parsley and garnish with the reserved red pepper and olives.

Serves: 4

Stuffed Cabbage

A 2-pound (1-kilogram) cabbage
1 quart water, lightly salted
2 cloves garlic
2 scallions (shallots), chopped
1 tablespoon margarine
1 tablespoon cream
4 eggs, separated

½ cup bread crumbs
1 tablespoon parsley, chopped
½ teaspoon salt
¼ teaspoon black pepper
Browned bread crumbs (optional)
Sour cream (optional)
Tomato juice (optional)

Set aside 6 outer cabbage leaves.

Cut the cabbage in quarters. Remove the hard, inner section. Boil the cabbage in 1 quart of salted water for 15 minutes. Drain and reserve the cooking liquid. Put the cabbage and the garlic through the grinder.

Sauté the scallions in margarine. Place the cabbage mixture in a large mixing bowl and add the scallions, cream, egg yolk, bread crumbs and parsley. Season with salt and pepper. Blend thoroughly. Whip the egg whites and fold into the cabbage mixture.

Divide the prepared mixture into 6 parts. Place each portion on a reserved cabbage leaf. Roll the leaves up (see page 130) and wrap them in pieces of muslin. Tie securely with kitchen string.

Place the cabbage bundles in the reserved cooking liquid. Cook over a low flame for 1 hour.

Serve with browned bread crumbs, sour cream or tomato juice.

Serves: 6

Carrot Pudding

1 pound (500 grams) carrots	4 tablespoons honey or orange
3 slices white bread, soaked in	marmalade
water and squeezed dry	1 teaspoon lemon juice
½ cup pecans, coarsely chopped	½ teaspoon brown sugar
1 tablespoon raisins	Rum
1 tablespoon currants	2 eggs, separated
1 tablespoon margarine,	
softened	

Grate the carrots finely. Mix with the bread. Add the pecans, raisins, currants, margarine and honey or marmalade. Blend thoroughly.

Season with lemon juice, brown sugar and salt. Add rum to taste. Beat the egg yolks and combine with the carrot mixture. Fold in the egg whites, whipped until stiff.

Place the pudding in a greased glass baking dish. Bake in a medium oven (350°) for 45 minutes.

Serves: 4

Baked Veal with Vegetables and *Tehina**

½ pound (250 grams) carrots, peeled and chopped
1 green pepper, seeded and cut into strips
¾ pound (375 grams) squash, peeled and cubed
¾ pound (375 grams) green peas, shelled
¾ pound (375 grams) potatoes, peeled and diced
2 stalks fennel, chopped
4 scallions (shallots), cut into rings

6 cloves garlic, minced
1 teaspoon salt
½ teaspoon black pepper
1 teaspoon paprika
2 pounds (1 kilogram) veal roast, sliced
1 medium slice avocado, mashed
¾ small can tomato paste
5 cups water
3 ounces (90 grams) margarine
3 tomatoes, chopped
¼ cup parsley, chopped

Mix together the carrots, pepper, squash, peas, potatoes, fennel and scallions. Add the garlic, salt, pepper and paprika. Place in a baking pan.

Coat the veal slices with avocado and add them to the pan.

Combine the tomato paste and water. Pour over the lamb and vegetable mixture. Dot with margarine and sprinkle with chopped tomato and parsley. Bake in a medium oven (350°) for 1 hour.

Accompany with a dish of *tehina*.

To prepare *Tehina*

½ can semi-prepared *tehina*
½ cup water
Juice of ½ lemon
2 teaspoons vinegar
6 cloves garlic, chopped

½ teaspoon salt
½ teaspoon paprika
1 tablespoon parsley, chopped
Black olives

Combine the semi-prepared *tehina,* water, lemon juice, vinegar, garlic and salt. Blend thoroughly.

Place the resulting mixture in a serving dish. Sprinkle with paprika and parsley. Garnish with black olives.

Serves: 4

* See page 20.

EGG and DAIRY DISHES

Banana Soufflé

5 large, firm ripe bananas
1½ tablespoons butter, softened
½ cup brown sugar
⅓ cup dry white wine
1 tablespoon lime juice
3 eggs, separated

Broil unpeeled bananas until soft, watching them carefully. Remove peels and press the flesh through a strainer. Add butter and sugar and beat well. Stir in the wine and lime juice. Beat the egg yolks and combine them with the banana mixture, mixing thoroughly. Beat the egg whites until stiff and fold in gently. Pour into a well-greased baking tin. Bake for 25 minutes in a medium oven (350°). Serve hot or cold.

Serves: 4-6

Spinach Omelet

½ pound (250 grams) fresh spinach
¼ cup parsley, finely chopped
½ onion, finely chopped
4 eggs
2 tablespoons matzo meal
1 tablespoon Parmesan cheese, grated
½ teaspoon salt
¼ teaspoon black pepper
⅛ teaspoon oregano
Pinch of saffron
⅓ cup oil

Rinse spinach well, remove stems and chop coarsely. Combine with the parsley, onion, eggs, matzo meal and cheese. Add the salt, pepper, oregano and saffron. Blend thoroughly. Heat the oil in an omelet pan. Cook the egg mixture on one side, taking care that it doesn't stick, flip over and cook on the other side. Serve at once.

Serves: 4

Fried Eggs and Vegetables

4 cloves garlic, crushed
1 teaspoon cumin
2 sticks (250 grams) margarine
2½ cups water
2 tablespoons tomato paste
½ teaspoon salt
¼ teaspoon black pepper
1 cup lentils
3 cups rice

½ pound (250 grams) scallions (shallots), chopped
1 medium tomato, chopped
1 green pepper, seeded, deribbed and diced
2 eggs
¾ cup Gouda cheese, grated
⅛ teaspoon nutmeg

Sauté the garlic and cumin in a large saucepan in 1½ sticks margarine. Add 2½ cups water, tomato paste, salt, pepper and lentils. Bring to the boil. Add the rice, cover tightly and continue boiling for 5 minutes. Lower the flame and cook an additional 20 minutes. Reserve.

Melt the remaining margarine in a large frying pan. Add the scallions, sauté, then add the tomato and green pepper. Lower the flame and cook 5 minutes.

Stir the eggs into the vegetable mixture. When they have solidified, sprinkle with grated cheese and nutmeg. Cook a few minutes more, stirring constantly. Serve at once.

Place the rice mixture on a flat dish. Top with the vegetable and egg.

Serves: 4

Eggs À La Sabra

6 eggs, hard-cooked
2 tablespoons *tehina* (for preparation see p. 20)
1 egg, beaten
½ teaspoon Worcestershire sauce

Cracker crumbs
Oil for deep-frying
6 large lettuce leaves
Green pepper rings
Black olives
Tomato slices

Cut the hard-cooked eggs in half, horizontally, and remove the yolks. Mash the yolks with the prepared *tehina* and return to their whites, reshaping into whole eggs. Dip them in the beaten egg to which the Worcestershire sauce has been added, then the cracker crumbs. Deep-fry in hot oil until golden. Serve on lettuce leaves. Garnish with green pepper rings, olives and sliced tomatoes.

Serves: 6

Deep-Fried Egg Puffs

1 cup flour	**½ teaspoon salt**
¾ cup lukewarm water	**½ teaspoon paprika**
Oil for deep-frying	**½ teaspoon oregano**
6 eggs	

Mix the flour and water. Knead well and let stand for 3 hours. Divide the dough into 6 pieces. Warm up a baking tin with a tightly fitting lid. When heated, grease the inner side of the lid with oil. Place a portion of dough in the tin and spread it out evenly. Replace the lid.

When the layer of dough has dried (about 1 minute) free it from the sides of the pan with a knife. Set aside to cool. Repeat this process with the other 5 dough sections.

Shape each prepared piece of dough into a 5-inch square. Fold over to form a triangle, pinching one side closed. Carefully insert a raw egg and a pinch of each of the seasonings into the open side of each pouch of dough and seal well. Deep-fry in hot oil. Serve piping hot.

Serves: 6

Hard-Cooked-Egg Soufflé

3 ounces (90 grams) margarine	**⅓ cup lemon juice**
1½ cups flour	**½ cup Parmesan cheese, grated**
1½ cups milk	**2 tablespoons cream**
½ teaspoon salt	**4 eggs, separated**
½ teaspoon paprika	**3 eggs, hard-cooked**
Pinch of nutmeg	

Melt the margarine and stir in the flour. Blend thoroughly. Gradually stir in the milk over a low flame. Remove from heat when the mixture becomes doughy but does not stick to the pan. Add the salt, paprika, nutmeg, lemon juice, cheese and cream. Combine well. Cool. Stir in the egg yolks, one by one. Beat the whites into a foam and fold gently into the mixture.

Grease a soufflé dish. Slice the hard-cooked egg yolks and grate the whites. Line the prepared soufflé dish with the sliced yolks and cover with the prepared cheese mixture. Sprinkle with the grated whites. Bake for ½ hour in a medium oven (350°).

Serves: 6

Eggs Poached in Bittersweet Sauce

1 tablespoon sugar	2 tablespoons currants
1 onion, sliced	1 clove
1 tablespoon oil	⅛ teaspoon black pepper
Juice of 1 lemon	6 eggs
2 cups water	1 tablespoon cornstarch
¼ teaspoon salt	(optional)
1 teaspoon brown sugar	4 cups rice, boiled

Heat the sugar and a few drops of water in a frying pan. Brown the sliced onion in oil and add to the sugar mixture with the lemon juice, water, salt, brown sugar, currants, clove and pepper. Bring to the boil.

Gently add the eggs, one by one. Be careful not to break the yolks. The cooking liquid may be thickened with 1 tablespoon cornflour, mixed with a little water (optional). When the eggs have solidified, drain and arrange on a bed of hot, boiled rice. Serve at once.

Serves: 6

Eggs in Wine Sauce

1 cup dry white wine	6 eggs
1 cup water	6 slices bread, toasted
¼ teaspoon salt	1 tablespoon chives, chopped
4 teaspoons flour	1 teaspoon paprika

Put the wine, water and salt in a frying pan. Bring to the boil. Stir in the flour, mixed with a little water, and blend thoroughly. Cook over a low flame, stirring constantly, until the sauce thickens.

Gently add the eggs, one by one. Be careful not to break the yolks. When the eggs have solidified, drain and place on the toast slices. Sprinkle with chives and paprika. Serve hot. Pass the sauce separately (optional).

Serves: 6

Spiced Eggs, Yemenite Style

1 onion, chopped
2 scallions (shallots), chopped
4 tablespoons margarine
3 eggs
3 stalks fennel, chopped
4 potatoes, diced
3 cloves garlic, crushed
1 can tomato paste
1½ cups water

¼ teaspoon soybean flour
⅛ teaspoon black pepper
⅛ teaspoon cayenne pepper
⅛ teaspoon cumin
Pinch of saffron
Pinch of ginger
Pinch of cinnamon
Pinch of ground cloves

Sauté the chopped onion and scallions in margarine until golden. Add the eggs and scramble lightly. Add the remaining ingredients, continuing to scramble, and cook over a low flame, stirring constantly, for 10 minutes.

Serves: 4

Minted Milk Balls

2½ quarts sour milk
Olive oil
Cinnamon

Cloves
Mint leaves

Put the sour milk into a clean, thick muslin bag and let it hang for 4 days. Take down the bag and shape the contents into small balls. Store them in a jar with olive oil, cinnamon, cloves and mint leaves.

Serve at breakfast.

Serves: 8

Noodles with Yogurt and Raisins

⅛ cup kidney beans
1 8-ounce (240-gram) package thin noodles
4 8-ounce (240-gram) containers unflavored yogurt

2 onions, chopped
2 scallions (shallots), chopped
2 tablespoons oil
1 cup currants
¾ cup water

Cook the kidney beans until soft. Drain and reserve.

Cook the noodles in salted water. Drain. Transfer to a large mixing bowl and stir in the yogurt, combining thoroughly. Let cool. Place on a serving plate.

Sauté the onions and scallions in oil until golden. Add the currants and sauté a few minutes more. Add water and simmer for 5 minutes. Drain.

Garnish the noodles with kidney beans and the currant mixture. Serve well chilled.

Serves: 8

Cheese *Borekas*

½ pint heavy cream
2¾ cups flour
¼ cup soybean flour
1½ sticks (200 grams) margarine
½ teaspoon salt
1 cup cottage cheese
½ cup Feta cheese, crumbled

2 eggs
2 tablespoons soybean flour
¼ teaspoon curry powder
¼ teaspoon paprika
1 egg, beaten
Sesame seeds

Combine the cream, flour, margarine and salt and knead into a smooth dough. Refrigerate overnight.

Roll out the dough to a thickness of ¼ inch. Cut into circles with the rim of a glass.

Prepare a filling by blending together the cheeses, 2 eggs, flour, curry and paprika. Mound onto the pastry circles and seal up the edges. Coat with beaten egg. Sprinkle with sesame seeds.

Arrange on a greased baking tin and bake in a hot oven (400°) for 20 minutes.

Serves: 6

Onion Soufflé

2½ ounces (75 grams) margarine
2½ tablespoons self-rising flour
1½ cups milk
1 tablespoon butter, salted
3 eggs, separated
1 teaspoon salt
¼ teaspoon paprika
⅛ teaspoon nutmeg
2 tablespoons parsley, finely chopped
Oil for frying
1 pound (500 grams) onions, sliced
Stuffed green olives

Heat the margarine in a saucepan. When it begins to bubble, stir in the flour. Blend well. Add the milk and continue to cook, stirring constantly, until the mixture thickens. Remove from the flame. Add the butter, egg yolks, salt, paprika, nutmeg and parsley. Blend thoroughly.

Heat the oil in a frying pan. Add the sliced onion. Sauté until golden. Cover the pan and cook a few minutes longer. Add to the egg-yolk mixture.

Whip the egg whites until firm. Fold them carefully into the onion mixture and transfer to a well-greased baking dish. Bake in a medium oven (350°) for ½ hour.

Serve at once, garnished with stuffed green olives.

Serves: 6

Cheese Pancakes

½ cup cottage cheese
¼ cup Feta cheese
1 egg
1 teaspoon onion, minced
1 tablespoon parsley, finely chopped
¼ teaspoon black pepper
Matzo meal
Oil for frying

Prepare a batter by combining the cheeses, egg, onion, parsley and pepper. Shape into individual pancakes. Coat with matzo meal on both sides. Fry in hot oil until golden. Serve at once.

Serves: 2

Pecan Coated Cheese Balls

1 pound (500 grams) Mozzarella cheese	½ teaspoon salt
	Dash of Worcestershire sauce
2 eggs	1 tablespoon parsley, finely chopped
2 tablespoons semolina	
3 tablespoons flour	6 tablespoons pecans, ground

Combine the cheese, eggs, semolina, flour, salt, Worcestershire sauce and parsley. Blend thoroughly. Set aside for ½ hour.

Shape the cheese mixture into balls. Cook for 10-15 minutes in boiling water. Drain.

Roll the cheese balls in the ground pecans until well coated.

Serves: 6

Carrot Pancakes

½ pint heavy cream	¼ teaspoon salt
2 eggs	¼ teaspoon cinnamon
1 tablespoon brown sugar	Oil for frying
½ cup flour	1 tablespoon matzo meal
¼ cup carrots, grated	1 tablespoon fine bread crumbs
½ teaspoon lemon rind, grated	

Combine the cream, eggs, sugar, flour, carrots, lemon rind, salt and cinnamon into a smooth batter. Heat the oil on a griddle and sprinkle with matzo meal and bread crumbs. Spoon the prepared pancake batter onto the griddle and cook. The meal and crumbs will prevent the pancakes from sticking to the griddle.

Serves: 2

Zucchini and Mushroom Soufflé

3 pounds (1½ kilograms)
zucchini (squash)
1 cup water, salted
3 tablespoons margarine
¼ cup flour
1 cup milk
4 eggs, separated

1 small can mushrooms, drained
and chopped
1½ cups Parmesan cheese,
grated
½ teaspoon salt
¼ teaspoon black pepper
¼ teaspoon oregano

Rinse the zucchini. Scrape but do not peel completely. Slice into ¼-inch thick pieces.

Place the sliced zucchini in a saucepan with 1 cup salted water. Cook over a low flame until the water comes to the boil. Drain the zucchini, reserving the cooking liquid.

Melt the margarine in a large saucepan. When it begins to bubble, stir in the flour, mixing well. Gradually incorporate the milk and the reserved cooking liquid, continuing to stir until the mixture thickens. Remove from the flame. Stir the egg yolks, one by one, into the prepared sauce. Blend thoroughly. Incorporate the mushrooms, reserved zucchini and 1 cup grated cheese. Season with salt, pepper and oregano. Gently fold in the egg whites, whipped until firm.

Place the prepared mixture in a greased baking dish. Sprinkle with the remaining grated cheese. Bake in a medium oven (350°) for 45 minutes. Serve at once.

Serves: 6

Spinach Soufflé

1 pound (500 grams) fresh spinach	4 eggs, separated
½ stick (60 grams) margarine	1 teaspoon onion, minced
¼ cup flour	½ teaspoon salt
1 cup milk	¼ teaspoon black pepper
1 cup Gouda cheese, grated	Dash of nutmeg

Rinse the spinach well. Remove the stems. Cook the spinach in boiling water, drain and put through a food mill.

Melt the margarine in a saucepan and stir in the flour. Blend thoroughly. Slowly add the milk, continuing to stir until the mixture thickens. Remove from the flame.

Add the spinach, cheese, egg yolks, onion and seasoning. Blend thoroughly. Whip the egg whites until stiff and fold them gently into the prepared mixture. Transfer the soufflé mixture to a greased soufflé dish. Bake in a moderate oven (350°) until done (about ½ hour).

Serves: 4

Cheese and Celery Soufflé

½ stick (60 grams) margarine	½ pound (250 grams) sharp
¼ cup flour	cheddar cheese
1 cup milk	½ cup celery, cooked, drained
½ teaspoon salt	and chopped
Pinch of nutmeg	4 eggs, separated

Melt the margarine in a saucepan and stir in the flour. Blend thoroughly. Slowly add the milk, continuing to cook and stir until the mixture thickens. Season with salt and nutmeg. Add the cheese and celery, mixing well.

Beat the egg yolks in a large mixing bowl. Gradually incorporate the cheese mixture. Whip the egg whites until stiff and fold them gently into the prepared mixture.

Transfer the soufflé mixture to a greased soufflé dish. Bake in a moderate oven (350°) for about 1 hour.

Serves: 4

DESSERTS

G

Pumpkin and Rice Jam

½ cup brown sugar
1 pound (500 grams) pumpkin,
peeled and finely grated
2 cups orange juice
1½ cups rice
½ teaspoon salt

Pinch of nutmeg
½ cup dry figs, thinly sliced
½ cup dates, pitted and thinly
sliced
¼ cup currants
Peel of 1 orange, grated

Melt the sugar over a low flame in a little water, stirring constantly to prevent burning. Add the pumpkin. Cover and cook slowly for ½ hour. Add the orange juice. Bring the mixture to the boil and stir in the rice, salt and nutmeg. Add the figs, dates, currants and orange peel and cook for an additional ½ hour. Accompany with sour cream sprinkled with cinnamon.

Serves: 4

Raisin Tart

1½ cups flour
2 ounces (60 grams) butter
2¼ cups milk
¼ teaspoon salt
6 eggs, separated

¾ cup sugar
½ teaspoon vanilla
1 cup raisins
½ cup pine nuts

Combine the flour, butter, ¼ cup milk and the salt and work into a smooth dough. Roll out and arrange in a greased baking tin.

Beat the egg yolks until light with half the sugar. Beat the whites into a foam with the remaining sugar. Gently add the yolks to the whites.

Add the vanilla, raisins and pine nuts to the remaining milk and mix into the egg mixture. Pour into the prepared pastry shell and bake for 1 hour in a medium oven (350°).

Serves: 4

Apple and Coconut Custard

3 cups milk
½ cup plus 2 tablespoons sugar
2 tablespoons prepared custard mix, diluted in a little cold milk
2 egg yolks
½ cup cream

2 large apples, peeled and cut into large chunks
1 teaspoon lemon juice
1 tablespoon margarine
Ladyfingers (sponge fingers)
2 tablespoons coconut, finely grated
1 cup cream, whipped

Boil the milk with ½ cup sugar. Add the diluted custard mix, stirring until the boiling milk thickens. Remove from flame and add the egg yolks and cream, stirring constantly. Reserve.

Steam the apple chunks with 2 tablespoons sugar, the lemon juice and the margarine.

Line the bottom of a glass dish with ladyfingers. Pour in ½ of the hot custard. Top with a layer of apple. Sprinkle on the coconut. Add another layer of ladyfingers and finish with the remaining custard. Refrigerate.

Immediately before serving, garnish with whipped cream.

Serves: 4

Whipped Apple Dessert

4 egg whites
1 cup sugar
1 teaspoon vinegar
1 teaspoon cornstarch
1 tablespoon cold apple juice

1 teaspoon vanilla
½ teaspoon cinnamon
2 tablespoons raisins
1 cup applesauce
½ cup pecans, slivered

Whip the egg whites into a thick foam. Carefully stir in ½ cup sugar, the vinegar, the cornstarch mixed with the apple juice and the vanilla. Whip again. Add the remaining sugar, continuing to whip into a thick, stiff foam.

Grease individual glass baking dishes and fill with the egg white mixture. Bake in a low oven (275°) for 1 hour. Remove from the oven and set aside to cool. Combine the cinnamon, raisins and applesauce and spread over the desserts. Sprinkle with slivered pecans.

Serves: 4

White Wine Custard

½ cup raisins
1½ cups Rhine wine, or another dry white wine
1 cup water
½ cup sugar

6-7 tablespoons prepared custard mix, diluted in ¼ cup water
1 egg, separated
Juice of ½ lime
Banana slices

Soak the raisins in water for ½ hour. Drain and reserve.

Bring the wine, water and sugar to the boil, stirring constantly. Combine the custard mix with the egg yolk and add to the boiling wine, stirring constantly. Cook over a low heat for 5 minutes, continuing to stir. Blend the lime juice into the custard mixture and remove from the flame.

Beat the egg white until stiff and fold it carefully into the prepared custard. Gently stir in the raisins.

Garnish with banana slices. Serve cold.

Serves: 4

Apples in Wine

½ cup currants
1 pound (500 grams) apples
¾ cup water
¾ cup sugar
⅛ teaspoon salt
2 tablespoons cornstarch

½ cup rosé wine
3 egg yolks
1 teaspoon vanilla
Pinch of nutmeg
Sweet seedless grapes

Soak the currants in water to cover for ½ hour. Drain.

Peel and quarter the apples. Cook them in water, sugar and salt in a saucepan until tender. Put through a food mill and return to the saucepan.

Make a paste of the cornstarch and wine. Stir it into the puréed apples and cook over a low flame, stirring constantly with a wooden spoon, for 10 minutes. Set aside to cool.

Beat in the egg yolks, vanilla and nutmeg. Stir until the mixture is smooth. Spoon into dessert bowls and garnish with grapes.

Serves: 6

Prickly Pear Purée

25-30 ripe prickly pears	2 tablespoons sugar
4 cups water	1 teaspoon cornstarch
Pinch of cloves	1 teaspoon cinnamon
1 teaspoon lemon juice	1 quart vanilla ice cream

Boil the pears in 4 cups water seasoned with cloves and lemon juice until the fruit falls apart. Drain.

Put the drained pears through a food mill. Transfer the resulting purée to a saucepan and bring to the boil, adding 2 tablespoons sugar and 1 teaspoon cornstarch, mixed with cold water, for every cup of purée. Boil for 2 minutes, stirring constantly.

Pour into individual dessert dishes and sprinkle with a mixture of sugar and cinnamon. Refrigerate.

Serve with vanilla ice cream.

Serves: 8

Jellied Wine Custard

6 egg yolks	⅓ cup warm water
¼ cup sugar	½ cup pecan meats (kernals)
2 cups dry white wine	½ cup cherries, pitted (stoned)
4 teaspoons gelatin	

Beat the egg yolks and sugar together until light. Add the white wine and blend thoroughly. Transfer to a saucepan and cook over a low flame, stirring constantly, until the mixture thickens. Do not boil.

Remove the thickened mixture from the flame. Add the gelatin, dissolved in warm water, stirring constantly. Continue to stir until the mixture cools. Transfer to a dessert mold, add the pecans and cherries and chill until firm. Turn out and serve.

Serves: 4

Tangerine Flan

3 cups tangerine juice
2 tablespoons lemon juice
1 cup water
6 tablespoons sugar
3 tablespoons prepared custard
mix, diluted in ½ cup water

1 teaspoon tangerine rind,
finely grated
1 egg, separated
Tangerine sections

Bring the juices, water and sugar to the boil. Stir in the custard mix and cook over a low flame, stirring constantly, for 2 minutes. Remove from heat. Incorporate the tangerine rind.

Whip the egg white. Add the yolk. Fold the egg mixture into the custard.

Serve cold in individual dishes, garnished with tangerine sections.

Serves: 2

Apples and Mangoes with Whipped Cream

2 pounds (1 kilogram) apples,
peeled and sliced
½ cup sugar
½ cup water
Juice of 1 lemon
1 teaspoon cinnamon

½ pound (250 grams) cake
crumbs
½ cup pine nuts
1 pound (500 grams) mangoes,
peeled and sliced
1½ cups cream, whipped

Place the apples, sugar, water and lemon juice in a large saucepan. Cook over a low flame until the apples are tender. Refrigerate.

Place the apple slices on a serving platter. Sprinkle with cinnamon, cover with ½ the cake crumbs and top with ½ the whipped cream. Add a layer of pine nuts, then a layer of mangoes, top with the remaining cake crumbs and finish with the rest of the whipped cream.

Garnish with fresh strawberries or cherries.

Serves: 6

Cinnamon Apple Pancakes

1 pound (500 grams) apples
2 cups flour
1 cup cold water
½ cup apple juice
6 tablespoons sugar
Peel of 1 lemon, grated

Pinch of salt
Oil for frying
1 ounce (30 grams) margarine,
in bits
2 teaspoons cinnamon

Peel the apples, cut into quarters and seed. Cut the seeded quarters into small pieces.

Combine the flour, water, apple juice, 4 tablespoons sugar, lemon peel and salt into a smooth batter. Add the apples and mix thoroughly.

Spoon the batter onto an oiled griddle. Bake the pancakes on both sides. Remove from heat, dot with margarine and sprinkle with the remaining sugar mixed with 2 teaspoons cinnamon. Serve at once.

Serves: 4

Baked Quince

Whole quinces, 1 per person   Margarine

Wash the quinces and dry them carefully, removing any outer hairs. Rub with margarine.

Bake in a medium oven (350°) for 2 hours, or until the quinces are tender and reddish brown.

The quinces can also be served stuffed, as follows:

Bread crumbs
Currants
Pine nuts

Lemon juice
Brown sugar

Bake the quinces as above. After 45 minutes, remove from oven and hollow them out. Combine the pulp with the above ingredients and return to the quince cases. Return to the oven and continue baking until tender.

Quince with Wine Sauce

5 large quinces	3 tablespoons sugar
1 cup dry vermouth	2 cups water
5 cloves	1 cup vanilla ice cream
½ teaspoon cinnamon	2 tablespoons chocolate bits
Juice of 1 lime	2 tablespoons coconut, grated

Cut the quinces in half. Remove the seeds and discard. Place the quinces in a pressure cooker. Add the vermouth, cloves, cinnamon, lime juice, sugar and water. Cook for 10 minutes.

Transfer to a baking pan and fill the centers with the liquids remaining in the pressure cooker. Pour the remaining liquid into the baking pan and bake in a medium oven (350°) for 15 minutes.

Chill. Fill the centers with ice cream, sprinkle with chocolate bits and coconut and serve at once.

Serves: 10

Cinnamon Jellied Baked Apples

6 large tart apples	1 package gelatin, black cherry-
6 teaspoons sugar	flavored
2 teaspoons raisins	2 cups water
1 teaspoon cinnamon	Fresh cherries

Core the apples. Combine the sugar, raisins and cinnamon and fill the core holes. Place in a greased baking dish and bake in a medium oven (350°) for about 45 minutes. Remove from the oven and set aside to cool.

Dissolve the gelatin in 2 cups hot water. Set aside to cool.

Place the apples in individual dessert bowls. Pour in the gelatin. Chill until firm. Garnish with cherries.

Serves: 6

Guavas Stuffed with *Tehina**

2 pounds (1 kilogram) guavas
4 tablespoons semi-prepared
tehina
¾ cup water

1½ cups figs, chopped
2 tablespoons coconut, shredded
3 tablespoons pine nuts
White grapes

Cut the guavas in half and hollow them out. Discard the pulp. Mix the semi-prepared *tehina* with ¾ cup water. Add the figs, coconut and pine nuts. Combine well. Fill the guava cases with the resulting mixture. Garnish with white grapes.

Serves: 4

*See page 20.

Lime Jellied Guavas

4 large guavas
1 package gelatin, lime-flavored
1 cup water
1 cup dry white wine

Juice of 1 lemon
Sugar to taste
Whipped cream

Cut the guavas in half and hollow them out. Reserve the pulp. Dissolve the gelatin in 1 cup hot water. Pour into the guava cases. Chill until firm.

Combine the guava pulp with the wine, lemon juice and sugar. Strain, to remove the seeds. Pour over the filled guava cases. Serve at once.

Accompany with whipped cream.

Serves: 4

Fried Bananas

5-6 semi-ripe bananas	Margarine
Salt and black pepper to taste	Brown sugar
Lime juice	Crushed walnuts

Peel the bananas and slice lengthwise. Sprinkle with salt, pepper and lime juice. Let stand for 1 hour.

Heat the margarine in a pan. Brown the bananas carefully, keeping them intact. Remove the bananas and sprinkle with brown sugar and crushed walnuts.

Serves: 4

Brandied Chocolate Delight

6 eggs, separated	3 tablespoons rum
1 cup sugar, scant	1 tablespoon strong coffee
5 ounces (150 grams) semi-sweet chocolate	Juice of 1 lemon
¼ cup cherry brandy	Crushed walnuts

Beat the egg yolks with ¼ cup sugar until smooth. Melt the chocolate in the top of a double boiler and add to the egg yolk mixture, stirring constantly.

Add the cherry brandy, rum, coffee and lemon juice.

Whip the egg whites until stiff, with the remaining sugar.

Fold carefully into the egg yolks and chocolate.

Spoon the pudding into 6 dessert dishes. Refrigerate for several hours. Sprinkle with crushed walnuts before serving.

Serves: 6

Apple Meringue with Custard Sauce

8 firm apples   ½ teaspoon Curaçao brandy
4 egg whites   ¼ teaspoon salt
⅔ cup sugar

Wash the apples well. Core and cook in boiling water until tender. Drain. Transfer to a baking dish.

Whip the egg whites until firm with ⅔ cup sugar, Curaçao brandy and the salt. Spoon over the apples and bake in a medium oven (350°) for 15 minutes. Prepare the sauce.

Sauce

1½ cups milk   4 egg yolks
½ teaspoon vanilla   3 tablespoons sugar
½ teaspoon almond extract

Boil the milk. Add the vanilla and almond extract.

Beat together the egg yolks and sugar. Transfer to a saucepan. Add the milk, stirring constantly. When the mixture has thickened, remove from the flame, set aside to cool and refrigerate.

Pass the sauce separately.

Serves: 8

Whipped Chocolate Brandy and Wine

3 ounces (90 grams) semi-   ½ cup sweet red wine
sweet chocolate   1 teaspoon cognac
3 tablespoons sugar   A few drops almond extract
4 eggs, separated

Melt the chocolate in the top of a large double boiler. Add the sugar, beaten egg yolks, wine, cognac and almond extract, beating constantly.

Whip the egg whites until firm and fold into the chocolate mixture.

Pour into individual dessert bowls and refrigerate.

Serves: 4

Sweet Rice

5 cups rice
8 cups water
1 cup sugar
2 teaspoons cinnamon

½ teaspoon lemon rind, grated
⅓ cup dates, chopped
1 cup walnuts, shelled and chopped
½ cup pine nuts, chopped

Place the rice in a large saucepan and cover with 8 cups of water. Add the sugar, cinnamon and lemon rind. Cook over a medium flame, stirring constantly, until the rice is cooked. Stir in the dates and heat through.

Serve hot in individual bowls, garnished with chopped walnuts and pine nuts.

Serves: 6

Sweet Potato Cake

2 pounds (1 kilogram) sweet potatoes
1 stick (125 grams) margarine
1 cup brown sugar
Juice of ½ lemon

½ teaspoon vanilla
¼ teaspoon almond extract
2 tablespoons cocoa
1 cup marshmallows, chopped
Grated chocolate

Peel the sweet potatoes and boil until tender. Drain. Transfer to a mixing bowl.

Add the margarine and brown sugar to the sweet potatoes. Cover, let stand until the margarine melts, then put the sweet potato mixture through a food mill. Add the lemon juice, vanilla and almond extract. Combine well. Divide the resulting mixture in half.

Add the cocoa to ½ the sweet potato mixture and beat until smooth. Stir in the marshmallows. Reserve.

Spread a clean damp towel on the table and spread ½ of the remaining sweet potato mixture (without the cocoa and marshmallows) on it. Reserve the remaining half. Cover with a second damp towel and press the sweet potato mixture into a flat layer. Remove the upper towel and cover the flattened layer of sweet potato with the sweet potato-cocoa-marshmallow mixture. Top with the reserved sweet potato.

Trim into a square or circle and turn out onto a platter. Sprinkle with grated chocolate, refrigerate for 1 hour and serve.

Serves: 6

Zenab Fingers

1 cup flour   2 tablespoons water
¼ teaspoon salt   Oil for frying
¼ cup sugar

Combine the flour, salt, sugar and water. Knead into a smooth dough. Roll the dough out into a thin layer and cut it into 4-inch squares. Fill each square with filling and roll it closed, shaping the edges to form "fingers". Fry the stuffed "fingers" in oil until golden, dip in syrup and serve at once.

Filling

¼ cup almonds, crushed   ½ teaspoon cloves
¼ cup raisins, finely chopped   ½ teaspoon nutmeg, freshly
½ cup sugar   grated
½ teaspoon cinnamon

Combine the above ingredients thoroughly.

Syrup

2 cups sugar   1 teaspoon lime juice
1 cup water   Apple juice

Bring the sugar and water to the boil. Add the lime juice and continue boiling until the mixture thickens. Remove from the flame and flavor with apple juice.

Serves: 6

206

Brandied Chocolate Cake

½ cup cocoa
¾ cup boiling water
1 teaspoon instant coffee
1¾ cups flour
1¾ cups sugar
1 tablespoon baking powder
½ teaspoon salt

½ cup oil
7 eggs, separated
1 teaspoon almond extract
½ teaspoon cream of tartar
½ teaspoon Kaluaha brandy
(coffee flavored)

Dissolve the cocoa in boiling water, stirring until no more bubbles form. Add the instant coffee and the brandy.

Combine the flour, sugar, baking powder and salt. Make a hole in the center of these dry ingredients and pour in the oil, egg yolks, almond extract and cocoa. Blend thoroughly.

Whip the egg whites with the cream of tartar until stiff. Fold into the prepared batter.

Transfer to a greased and floured baking pan. Bake in a medium oven (350°) until done (about ½ hour).

Serves: 6

Dried Fruit Stuffed with Cream Cheese

Dried fruit; prunes, dates, apricots
Ricotta cheese

Grated coconut
Shelled walnuts

Wash the fruit and steam it over hot water in a covered colander for about 15 minutes (or until tender). Set aside to cool.

Make a lengthwise slit in each piece of fruit. Remove the pits (stones) and fill with Ricotta cheese sprinkled with coconut.

Garnish each stuffed fruit with a walnut.

Orange Cake

1 orange, squeezed and unpeeled
1 cup currants
⅓ cup pecans, shelled
2 cups flour
¼ teaspoon club soda
1⅓ cups sugar

1 stick (125 grams) margarine
1 cup milk
2 eggs
5 tablespoons orange juice
1 tablespoon lemon juice
1 teaspoon cinnamon

Put the orange, currants and pecans through the grinder.

Combine the flour, club soda and 1 cup sugar. Add the margarine and ¾ cup milk. Mix for 2 minutes, add the eggs and the remaining milk and mix for 2 minutes more. Carefully incorporate the orange and nut mixture.

Grease and flour a baking tin with margarine. Pour in the batter and bake in a medium oven (350°) for 45 minutes.

Remove the cake from the oven and while it is still hot pour on the orange juice mixed with lemon juice. Sprinkle with the remaining sugar, combined with the cinnamon.

Serves: 6

Honey Cake

7 eggs, separated
1 cup sugar
¾ cup honey
2 cups flour, sifted
1 tablespoon orange rind, grated

1 teaspoon cloves
½ teaspoon cinnamon
⅛ teaspoon cardamon
Dry brown sugar

Whip the egg whites with ½ the sugar until stiff. Reserve.

Beat the egg yolks with the remaining sugar and honey until light. Fold in the whipped whites, flour, orange rind and spices.

Grease and flour a deep baking pan. Bake in a medium oven (350°) for 40 minutes. Set aside to cool. Sprinkle with brown sugar.

Serves: 6

Orange Cheese Tart

2 cups flour	1 cup cottage cheese
3 ounces (90 grams) margarine	7 tablespoons orange juice
1¼ cups sugar	1 tablespoon lime juice
1 egg yolk	2 eggs

Prepare a crust with the flour, margarine, ⅓ cup sugar and the egg yolk. Use it to line a greased baking pan.

Combine the cottage cheese, orange juice, lime juice, remaining sugar and 2 eggs.

Beat thoroughly. Spoon onto the tart shell and bake in a medium oven (350°) for 40 minutes or until golden. Remove from the oven. Cool. Prepare the topping.

Topping

1 cup orange juice	½ teaspoon Curaçao brandy
½ cup sugar	1 teaspoon coconut, grated
1 tablespoon orange marmalade	Orange sections

Put the orange juice, sugar, marmalade and brandy in a saucepan. Bring to the boil and cook, stirring constantly, until the mixture thickens. Remove from the flame, add the coconut and spread over the tart. Garnish with orange sections.

Serves: 6

Yellow Cake

10 eggs, separated
1¾ cups sugar
4 tablespoons flour

1 teaspoon vanilla
½ teaspoon almond extract
2 tablespoons water

Beat the egg yolks with 4 tablespoons sugar for 10 minutes. Add the flour, vanilla and almond extract. Mix thoroughly and pour into a greased baking tin. Bake in a medium oven (350°) for 20 minutes.

While the cake is baking, beat 1 cup sugar into the egg whites until stiff. Reserve. 5 minutes before the cake is done, remove it from the oven, cover it with the whipped egg whites and return it to the oven.

Brown the remaining sugar in a saucepan. Add 2 tablespoons boiling water and remove from the flame. When the cake has finished baking and the meringue is crusty and golden, pour on the sugar mixture and set aside to cool.

Serves: 8

Cheese Cake with Cognac

3 ounces (90 grams) margarine
1½-2 cups sugar
8 eggs, separated
2 pounds (1 kilogram) Ricotta cheese
1½ teaspoons vanilla

2 teaspoons cognac
2 tablespoons cornstarch
⅓ cup currants
4 tablespoons walnut meats
Peel of 1 lemon, grated

Cream the margarine and ½ the sugar. Beat the egg yolks until light and add to the margarine-sugar mixture. Beat in the cheese, vanilla, cognac, cornstarch, currants, walnuts and lemon peel. Combine thoroughly.

Whip the egg whites until stiff with the remaining sugar. Fold into the cheese mixture.

Bake in a greased and floured pan in a medium oven (350°) for 1 hour.

Serves: 6

Orange-Flavored Dough

7 ounces (210 grams) margarine   1 tablespoon lime juice
3 cups flour   ¼ teaspoon salt
1 cup orange juice

Combine the margarine and flour, add the remaining ingredients and work into a dough. Knead well. Roll into a ball and refrigerate for several hours. This dough can be rolled out as a pie crust or filled to make dumplings. It is especially good with ground meat, liver, eggplant, mushroom, fish and apple dishes.

Rum Sweet Loaf ("Basbousa")

5 cups sugar   Warm water
2 cups margarine, melted   1 teaspoon vanilla
½ teaspoon salt   ½ teaspoon almond extract
5 pounds (2½ kilograms) semolina

Combine the sugar and margarine. Add salt, semolina and enough warm water to make a soft dough. Add the vanilla and almond extract and knead thoroughly.

Place the dough in a square, greased baking tin. Bake in a medium oven (350°) until the top is golden. Remove from oven and cut into squares immediately.

Place the squares in individual dessert bowls and cover with syrup. Serve at once.

Syrup

2 cups sugar   1 tablespoon lemon juice
1 cup water   ¼ cup rum

Bring the sugar and water to the boil. Add the lemon juice and cook, stirring constantly, until the mixture thickens. Remove from the flame, cool and add the rum.

Serves: 8

Orange Meringue Pie

3 cups flour
7 ounces (210 grams) margarine
¾ cup plus 1 tablespoon sugar
1½ teaspoons baking powder
2 cups orange juice
1 tablespoon lime juice

4 tablespoons cornstarch
¼ teaspoon salt
1 teaspoon lemon rind, grated
3 oranges, divided into sections
3 egg whites

Combine the flour, margarine, 6 tablespoons sugar and the baking powder. Line a greased and floured baking tin with this mixture. Bake in a medium oven (350°) until golden. Set aside to cool.

Bring the orange juice, lime juice and 4 tablespoons sugar to the boil. Add the cornstarch, mixed with water, and cook over a low flame, stirring constantly, until the mixture thickens. Mix in the salt and lemon rind. Remove from the flame.

Cover the prepared crust with orange sections and spoon on the orange pudding. Top with the egg whites, whipped stiff with the remaining sugar. Return to the oven and bake until the meringue is golden.

Serves: 6

Creamy Apple and Pear Roll

2 cups cottage cheese
1 cup plain yogurt
2 apples, peeled, cored and mashed
2 pears, peeled, cored and mashed
½ teaspoon cinnamon

¼ teaspoon lemon peel, grated
2 teaspoons sugar
½ teaspoon almond extract
Walnut halves
Orange slices
Raisins

Combine the cottage cheese and yogurt in a mixing bowl. Add the mashed apple, pears, cinnamon, lemon peel, sugar and almond extract, blending thoroughly.

Shape the cheese mixture into the form of a roll. Garnish with walnut halves. Transfer to a serving platter. Surround with orange slices sprinkled with raisins.

Serves: 4

Rum Nut Squares

Puff paste   3 ounces (90 grams) margarine, melted

Roll out the puff paste and divide into 2 12-inch squares. Place the first square on a greased baking sheet and cover with the filling. Top with the remaining square of dough.

Indent the surface of the top dough layer with a sharp knife, to form 6 2-inch squares. Coat with melted margarine. Bake in a moderate oven (325°) until the top layer is golden. Remove from oven. Separate squares with a knife and cover with syrup immediately.

Filling

1½ cups walnuts, crushed   ¼ teaspoon nutmeg, freshly
¼ cup brown sugar   ground
    ¼ teaspoon cinnamon

Combine the above ingredients thoroughly.

Syrup

2 cups sugar   1 teaspoon lemon juice
1 cup water   Rum to taste

Bring the sugar and water to the boil. Add the lemon juice. Continue to cook, stirring constantly, until the syrup thickens. Remove from the flame and flavor with rum to taste.

Serves: 6

Tangy Carrot Cookies

⅓ cup carrots, grated ¼ teaspoon salt
½ teaspoon ginger 2 cups flour
2 eggs ⅓ cup orange juice
2 sticks (250 grams) margarine 1 teaspoon lemon rind, grated
⅓ cup sugar ½ teaspoon vanilla

Combine the above ingredients into a dough. For cookies, place teaspoonsful of dough on a greased baking sheet and bake in a medium oven (350°) for about 10 minutes.

The dough may also be rolled out, filled with cheese, rolled closed, dipped in flour and baked in a medium oven (350°) until brown.

Cheese filling

1½ pounds (750 grams) cream ⅓ cup sugar
cheese 2 tablespoons dates, chopped
½ cup milk ½ teaspoon vanilla
2 eggs, separated 1 tablespoon flour

Combine the cream cheese and milk. Add the egg yolks, then the whites whipped with sugar. Stir in the remaining ingredients and mix well.

Serves: 4

Rose Hip Jelly

2 pounds (1 kilogram) rose 4 cups brown sugar
hips 1½ cups water
Juice of 2 limes Food coloring (optional)

Rinse the rose hips thoroughly. Sprinkle with lime juice and sugar and allow to stand overnight. Put the hips through a grinder.

Bring the sugar and water mixture to the boil. Add the rose hips and cook, stirring constantly, for 15 minutes. Set aside to cool then store in glass jars. Color with red food coloring if so desired.

Brandied Rice Pudding

3 cups milk
1 cup water
1¾ cups rice
3 tablespoons vanilla
2 teaspoons almond extract
⅔ cup sugar
3 bananas, peeled
2 persimmons, peeled and seeded

2 apples, peeled, cored and seeded
2 tangerines, peeled and seeded
1 teaspoon cherry brandy
½ pint cream
3 tablespoons grated coconut
3 tablespoons pine nuts

Scald the milk. Add the water, rice, vanilla and almond extract. Cover and cook over a low flame until the rice is tender but not completely cooked. Reserve 2 tablespoons of the sugar and add the rest to the rice mixture. Bring to the boil. When the rice is cooked through, set it aside to cool in a mixing bowl.

Blend the prepared fruit in a blender. Add the brandy and remaining sugar, combining thoroughly. Mix the fruit purée with the reserved rice. Transfer to a serving dish.

Before serving, pour the cream over the rice pudding. Garnish with grated coconut and pine nuts.

Serves: 4

Tehina and Nut Balls

6 cups flour
2 cups margarine
½ cup sugar
½ cup warm water

¼ teaspoon salt
1 egg yolk, beaten
Sesame seeds

Combine the above ingredients and knead into a dough. Divide the dough into 4-inch squares or 4-inch-wide circles. Fill each section with 1 tablespoon filling, seal closed and flatten between your palms. Arrange in a greased baking tin. Coat with beaten egg yolk. Sprinkle with sesame seeds and bake in a medium oven (350°) for ½ hour.

Filling

1 pound (500 grams) walnuts, ground
2 tablespoons dates, chopped
3 ounces (90 grams) sesame seeds

1 teaspoon cinnamon
½ cup prepared *tehina* (for preparation, see page 20)

Combine the above ingredients into a smooth mixture.

Serves: 6

Nut Cookies

1 pound (500 grams) walnuts, ground
1½ cups brown sugar
5 grains cardamon, freshly ground

Pinch of cloves
½ teaspoon lemon juice
2 egg whites
½ cup apple juice
2 tablespoons potato flour

Combine the walnuts, sugar, cardamon, cloves, lemon juice and egg whites. Work into a smooth dough. If the dough is too stiff, thin with apple juice.

Form the dough into small balls and place on a baking sheet dusted with **potato flour. Bake for 15 minutes in a medium oven (350°).**

Serves: 6

DRINKS

Brandied Orange Punch

6 cups orange juice
¾ cup sugar
6 cups strong tea
Juice of 2 lemons

Orange sections
Cloves
1 cup peach brandy

Heat the orange juice and sugar together. Combine with the tea and lemon juice.

Stud the orange sections with cloves. Place in the punch mixture. Stir in the peach brandy, chill and serve.

Serves: 12

Very Hot Lemon Punch

5 lemons
1 cup tea
2 cups sugar
1 nutmeg, crushed
5 cups boiling water

1 cup rum or cognac
1 bottle dry red wine
Lime slices
Pineapple slices

Peel and squeeze the lemons. Cook the peels in the tea, sugar and nutmeg for 15 minutes. Add the lemon juice.

Strain the resulting mixture into a large, heatproof container. Add the boiling water, rum or cognac and wine. Serve very hot with slices of lime and pineapple.

Serves: 6

Apple Wine Punch

12 small apples
1¼ cups sugar
1 teaspoon cinnamon
1 teaspoon pecans, chopped
1½ cups orange juice

¼ cup tangerine syrup
Juice of 1 lemon
2 cups dry red wine
1 cup tea

Peel and core the apples. Put 1 teaspoon sugar into each core hole. Place the apples in a baking dish and bake in a medium oven (350°) for ½ hour.

Combine the remaining sugar, cinnamon, pecans and the liquids. Heat over a low flame (do not boil) for 15 minutes.

Place an apple in each of 12 individual punch cups and cover with the hot wine mixture.

Serves: 12

INDEX

with Spinach, 25
Chicken
in Apple and Brandy
Sauce, 62
with Apple Casserole, 64
and Asparagus Salad, 82
Baked, and Bananas, 69
Baked Stuffed, 67
in Barbecue Sauce, 70
Braised, with Wine and Mush-
rooms, 66
Broth, Minted, 47
Canapés with Quince, 72
Cups, 79
Curried, Pot Pie, 75
Curried in Wine, 63
Deep-dish, in "Tangerine Cham-
pagne" Sauce, 77
in Honey and Orange Juice, 71
Honeyed Balls with Rum, 81
Israeli Stuffed, 85
Lemon-flavored, 66
with Lima Beans and Mush-
rooms, 63
Liver Balls, 88
Liver Canapés and *Tehina,* 78
Livers with Mushrooms in
Wine, 89
Liver and Rice Balls, 89
Livers with Stuffed Quince, 90
and Pecan Doughnuts, 74
Pie with Walnuts, 61
in Pineapple and Cherry Sauce,
64
and Pomegranate Soup, 55
and Potato Pie, 84
Red Wine Kebabs, 84
Roast Stuffed, in Pomegranate
Sauce, 60
Roast, Stuffed with Quince, 86
Rolls in Wine Sauce, 70
Sautéed, with Pomegranates, 74
and Scallions, Yemenite Style,
71
Smothered, with Corn and
Olives, 80
Soup, Lemon-flavored, 45
Stuffed with Cauliflower, 68
Stuffed Fried, 76
Sweet Potato and Vegetable
Pancake, 176
Sweet and Sour, 65
and *Tehina* Pie, 83
and Vegetable Casserole, 87
and Vegetable Stew, 61
and Walnut Balls, 75
and Walnuts, Zucchini Stuffed
with, 172
in Wine, 59

Chocolate
Brandy and Wine, Whipped,
204
Cake, Brandied, 207
Delight, Brandied, 203
Cinnamon
Apple Pancakes, 200
Jellied Baked Apples, 201
Coconut and Apple Custard, 196
Codfish
with Chick Peas, 118
Israeli Style, 121
and Mushrooms, 120
Paprikash, Hungarian Style,
116
Roll, 122
Cold
Fish in Spicy Lemon Juice, 105
Stuffed Fish, 113
Turkey Salad, 96
Cookies
Nut, 216
Tangy Carrot, 214
Corn
Pudding, Baked, 27
Soup, 47
Couscous with Beef Goulash, 143
Creamy Apple and Pear Roll,
212
Cucumber/s
with Beet Soup, 56
Salad, 29
Soup, 50
Curried
Avocado and Eggplant Salad,
35
Beef Salad, Tomatoes Stuffed
with, 32
Chicken Pot Pie, 75
Chicken in Wine, 63
Eggs, Eggplant Stuffed with,
173
Fish and Rice, 109
Custard
Apple and Coconut, 196
Jellied Wine, 198
Sauce, 204
White Wine, 197
Deep-dish Chicken, 77
Deep-fried
Egg Puffs, 185
Fish Balls, 101
Dough
Orange-Flavored, 211
Potato, 168
Doughnuts, Chicken and Pecan,
74
Dried Fruit Stuffed with Cream
Cheese, 207

Dumpling, Stuffed Brain, 150
Egg/s
Carp, Sautéed, 115
Curried, Eggplant Stuffed
with, 173
and Fish Rolls, 100
Fried, and Vegetables, 184
Poached in Bittersweet Sauce,
186
Puffs, Deep-fried, 185
à la Sabra, 184
Soufflé, Hard-cooked, 185
in Wine Sauce, 186
Yemenite Style, Spiced, 187
Eggplant/s
and Baked Fish, 124
Baked, with Potatoes, 163
Casserole, 157, 160
with Cheese, 160
and Curried Avocado Spread, 35
Fish Stuffed with, 114
and Lamb Patties, 142
Patties, 158
and Pickle Rolls, 38
Pickled, 19
Pie, Baked, 170
and Pimiento Pie, 170
Quarters, Filled, 166
Salad, with Cheese, 33
Stuffed, 161
Stuffed with Cheese, 162
Stuffed with Curried Eggs, 173
Stuffed with Lamb, 153
Tomatoes Stuffed with, 173
Falafel, 25
Fennel Logs Stuffed with Calf's
Liver, 148
Figs with Lamb, 145
Filled Eggplant Quarters, 166
Fish
and Apricots, 120
Baked, with Cheese, 113
Baked, and Eggplant, 124
Baked in Pomegranate Juice
and Wine, 116
Baked, in *Tehina,* 106
Baked in Wine, 105
Balls, Deep-fried, 101
Cakes with White Wine, 100
Cold, in Spicy Lemon Juice, 105
Cold, Stuffed, 113
Curried, and Rice, 109
and Egg Rolls, 100
Fillets Baked in Tomato Sauce,
108
Fried, Spanish Style, 118
Fried, in *Tehina,* 107
n'Milk Stew, 108
Minted, 110